T0158781

IMAGE
SCRIMMAGE

9 Ways Women Win with Body Language

DR. DONNA VAN NATTEN

IMAGE SCRIMMAGE
9 WAYS WOMEN WIN WITH BODY LANGUAGE

iUniverse books may be ordered through booksellers or by contacting:

iUniverse
1663 Liberty Drive
Bloomington, IN 47403
www.iuniverse.com
1-800-Authors (1-800-288-4677)

ISBN: 978-1-5320-0756-9 (sc)
ISBN: 978-1-5320-0754-5 (hc)
ISBN: 978-1-5320-0755-2 (e)

Library of Congress Control Number: 2016915512

Print information available on the last page.

iUniverse rev. date: 09/24/2016

ACKNOWLEDGEMENTS

To my children - who are my being
To my parents – who are my unwavering
To my significant – for making me feel like a diamond
Always.

CONTENTS

FOREWORD

"The body never lies" – *Martha Graham*

Long before Donna approached me about contributing to this book, I was aware of the very talented American dancer/choreographer Martha Graham via my daughter who has been a dancer since she learned to walk. Little did I know that famous quote above would leap into my head as I sat down to write this Foreword. It was the perfect quote given the focus of this book, and I knew I had to include it as a "kickoff" to my opening comments.

I share Donna's interest and training in the social sciences and have always been fascinated by the amount of information one can discern from nonverbal communication. In fact, like many of you, I utilize my skill set in reading nonverbal communication on a daily basis in my interactions with students, faculty, administrators, athletes, and coaches. As is the case with all skill sets, however, not everybody possesses the ability to read nonverbal communication to the same degree, which is the reason, I suspect, that you have purchased this book.

The good news is that you are holding the best resource that exists on the topic of empowering women via knowledge of workplace nonverbal communication. This book, written by a friend and colleague I've known for over 30 years, effectively merges the experiences of professional women with research and data to provide readers with knowledge and skills that they can immediately put into practice. While you will not get bogged down by detailed research reviews, Donna has provided the reader with documented support for her statements and recommendations. So, if you are eager to learn more about a particular topic in one of the chapters, you will have a number of references at your disposal to use as a starting point.

While this book is grounded in research and data, the primary focus, value, and strength of the book is in its application to real-world situations that the reader is likely to experience in her or his professional life. In addition to Dr. Van Natten, you will meet and learn from a number of women throughout this book who have utilized their knowledge of nonverbal communication to succeed in their chosen fields. As you begin to absorb the material in this book, however, you are likely to ask yourself the following question – if we recognize the benefits of being able to effectively read the nonverbal communication of others, and if this is a skill that we can learn, why don't more people devote their time and energy to improving these skills? The answer likely lies in the norms of our culture. Let me provide a brief analogy that may help clarify this statement.

Part of my background includes working with athletes to enhance their psychological skills during, and in preparation for, their performances. Much like the debate regarding the percentage of communication that is verbal vs. nonverbal (some experts claim that as much as 93% of all communication is nonverbal), sport scientists engage in constant debate over the percentage of athletic success that is due to mental vs. physiological factors. Ultimately, of course, the percentages are irrelevant. Even if, for the sake of argument, we assume that nonverbal communication makes up a relatively small portion of all communication, the potential impact of missing out on even 10% of the information being conveyed can be devastating. In the world of athletics, failing to adequately train the mind can have equally negative consequences on performance but, yet, few coaches devote practice time to mental training and far too few athletes commit even a fraction of their training time to improving their psychological skills. Hopefully, the analogy is becoming clear now – how much time and effort have you expended to enhance your understanding and practice of effective verbal communication (sending and receiving verbal messages) compared to aspects of nonverbal communication? Habit, history, and tradition dictate much of our behavior. Mindsets are exceedingly difficult to change. Every now and then we need a shock to the system and you will, no doubt, experience this in any workshop that Donna leads on the topic of women, empowerment, and nonverbal behavior. Fortunately, she has produced a literary "aftershock" that goes into far greater depth than she is able to provide in a workshop format.

Truly great training books open our eyes, stretch our mind, and provide a blueprint for actionable steps that remain once the initial surge of motivation has diminished. Thanks to Donna and her team of experts, you are holding in your hands the blueprint that will allow you to effectively glean important information via nonverbal communication. Before you flip another page, however, I would offer one suggestion to you – do NOT read the entire book all at once. Should you choose to do so, you may find yourself so overwhelmed with a desire to attend to the many aspects of nonverbal communication that you will, paradoxically, miss out on much of it, including what is actually being said. Instead, try to incorporate information and skills from one or two chapters at a time into your personal interactions.

In the 1987 movie *Wall Street*, Michael Douglas (as character Gordon Gekko) utters the memorable line "The most valuable commodity I know of is information." Given this, it should be clear to all of us that a firm grasp of nonverbal communication is not just a *preferable* skill set to possess - it is an absolutely *critical* one. Whether in athletic, academic, business, or social settings, we find ourselves routinely engaged in levels of competition in which the slightest advantage can make all the difference in the world. If you have ever said to yourself or others that "I'll do anything in order to _____," this book is your wake-up call. An untapped and abundant resource exists with the potential to empower you in the workplace. With this book, Dr. Donna Van Natten has created a roadmap that will allow you to navigate the precarious domain of your professional relationships. Get in the driver's seat - you will soon find your personal interactions to be far more satisfying and meaningful than you do today. Enjoy the journey!

Curt L. Lox, Dean

INTRODUCTION

BODY LANGUAGE AND NON-VERBAL COMMUNICATION

While still considered by many to be a man's world, it cannot and should not be discounted that 57% of today's workforce are women, 56% of females account for undergraduate college enrollment, and a record 40% constitute heads of households. The data speaks for itself in that we, as "breadwinners, and homemakers, and pattycakemakers" are making economic and social contributions at both our workplaces and communities.

From social scenes to workplace meetings, a woman's role is not static. Her corporate presence is growing and requires nurturing. Women's groups, entrepreneurial workshops, and diversity trainings readily available in some cities, but scarce in others, bring to light the critical need for helping others – in particular, women. As the faces of our emerging Millennial managers appears to get more youthful from the perception of fellow Gen X and other professionals, a progressive mindset acknowledges this and embraces the opportunities.

It remains my continuous observation that women of all ages and stages are unique in how we contribute to our communities and careers by how we communicate, control ourselves (or lack thereof), and use our non-verbal actions, tone of voices, and words.

Our strides are noteworthy. We are tapping on the glass ceiling … and it's shattering into a beautiful menagerie of glistening diamonds! Women have come a long way on the path to inclusion and equality; hopefully, not at the expense of men, but rather with the inclusion of them. If we want to better understand how we, as independent and gifted women, can continue to capitalize on our successes and advances, then hard, honest conversations, statistical trends analyses, gaps and reality checks, and emotional occupational hazard reviews are in order. I presume you're RSVPing to attend.

From the 5.1 million married women with incomes greater than their spouses, to the 8.6 million single mothers burning the life and work candle at both ends, we should dive deeper to better understand these women and learn from their trailblazing stories. The fact remains that we need to continue to stretch our strides, shatter those ceilings, and ensure that our mothers, wives, friends, sisters, and daughters (and the fathers, partners, guys, brothers, and sons who unapologetically support us) thrive while living their dreams.

designed by freepik.com

Since you now have this book in your hand (or on an e-platform), you are taking an active role in learning more about yourself and how you want to navigate your world and live your dreams. For every man reading this, diving deep for pearls, and extracting diamonds, congratulations on recognizing the value of women and understanding the impact they have in shaping your life. We think you're a gem, too!

This guide stands ready to channel our smart minds on such a journey, and I want you to view this as an informative tool to share with others who may need a little bit of polish or a little understanding to shine. Filled with "research-light," used intentionally to keep statistics and overwhelming data from engulfing our brains, it is my intention to share some of the available wealth leading, guiding, stereotyping, and reinforcing who we are and, perhaps, why we are where we are. Large spoonfuls of humor and wit help the truths and frustrations go down a little easier.

Chapter titles speak for themselves and each section offers ideas and ponderings for the open mind in learning mode. You may not agree with some of the research, struggle with the viewpoints of experts doing the fieldwork, and I concur. I continue to challenge the status quo in my world, and will admit that knowledge is powerful. I know how I want my intelligence and image displayed on social billboards.

A mountain of research from content experts and academics committed to the work are included because data drives workplace decisions. In today's accountability and ROI-driven workplaces, value goes beyond good character, or so it seems. It encompasses workplace investments; and decision makers demand a solid return. Research sources are cited at the end of the book; I invite you to grab a latte or something a little heartier after a day's work, and read a journal article or two of interest to you. These validated resources arm us with information to grow our brains, challenge our mental constructs, and brand ourselves.

Each chapter concludes with Take-Aways and visuals to enhance the message. Captivating Sage Stories add depth, personal experiences, application, and pearls of wisdom from women (and the men who support us) who practice what they preach add both depth and perspective. I profusely thank each of these professionals for taking the time to share their unique perspectives. When I first received their contributions, my eyes eagerly drank in their reflections and advice. I was, and remain, a proud and humbled colleague.

Finally, at the start of your path or somewhere in between, I make you aware that you will read about sensitive body parts, animal behaviors mirroring human behaviors, controlled and uncontrollable emotions, and the perceptions of others surrounding you. Sometimes these differences about us are difficult to accept; we want to be known and respected only for our minds and contributions without reference to gender distinctions. Differences between the two genders will be discussed because, the fact is, we are two genders. We are the **Fe** in **Female**. For those Chemistry majors and lab lovers, that means that we are made of Iron. Darn right!

An awareness of both your personal self and social self, hopefully, will be enriched by what you read, laugh at, wonder about, and share with other people. A little knowledge and fun body language trivia is always a hit in a social situation. Remember, nonverbal communication and predictive or reactive behavior happens in clusters, not isolation. As observers who love people watching, process the scene like a good detective. A scratch of the nose isn't always deception. A step back is not the only indicator of one's thoughts fleeing from the scene. Finger chewing isn't the only sign for insecurity.

designed by freepik.com

As primary visual receivers of information, begin to take note of how our other senses play a significant role in nonverbal communication. Does something smell fishy when you walk into a meeting? Do the little hairs on your skin stand erect when you interact with certain (you know, "creepy") people? Do certain odors trigger a childhood memory or immediately make your nose crinkle in disgust? Recognizing how our own bodies and minds react are subtle, and effective, clues to how we communicate and glean valuable information from our environment. Don't forget, this works the other way, too. Others are watching us, taking in our own nonverbal behaviors, and drawing conclusions for authentic messaging as part of the 7/38/55 rule for words, tone of voice, and body language driving how we navigate our world. Bon voyage, captains!

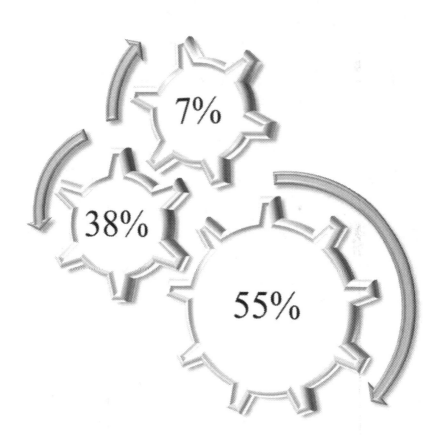

Sage Story

A Meaningful Life by Dana Stark

I work in the field of education and was raised in a family of nurses, teachers, and scientists. I was extremely fortunate to be raised by strong female role models and men who believed in me. My maternal grandmother worked as a nurse and raised 3 children while my grandfather was deployed in Korea and World War II. She was a proud, educated woman who raised 3 children. In turn, these children went out in the world as educators and environmentalists.

My mother had high expectations of two her daughters, raising us to contribute positively to society, be compassionate, creative, as well as independent. She never said, "If you go to college…" It was always, "When you go to college." My mother cared for us deeply, but she also had her own life. Although, we grumbled at times about her not packing our lunches, not being our own personal taxi driver to activities, not solving our spats with friends, and never allowing us to wimp out because of a difficulty, like my sister's diabetes. We now recognize she enabled us to be who we are today.

We were able to care for ourselves, handle disappointments, rally from the blows of life; and make sure not to lose ourselves in the craziness of day-to-day life. The women on my mother's side of the family were mothers AND career women. They worked hard, were fiercely loving, and honest. All faced adversity along the way, but it was always dealt with grace and determination. Anytime my grandmother was faced with a challenge or a seemingly insurmountable blow, and there were many, she would say, "This, too, shall pass."

When I was 16, I found that I was losing my hearing in my left ear from a hereditary degenerative hearing loss. Prior to this discovery, my mother was often frustrated at my seemingly 'lack of attention.' I began to develop a hyper-vigilance in public - so as not to call attention to myself for not noticing someone was talking to me. Facial expressions, eye contact, body language, and lip-reading were extremely useful. At one point, I tried amplification, but was not ready to accept that I needed help. Nor did I know what I was missing.

In college, I was able to succeed without interventions for several years, studying speech-language pathology. Building relationships with my professors, TA's, and classmates was extremely important for my success because they cared about my achievements. My hearing, though, began to significantly deteriorate in my right ear towards the end of my Bachelor's degree work. I was struggling to hear the questions and comments from others in classes. I was reluctant to participate in whole class discussions because it was embarrassing to ask the same question or make the same comment.

While in school, I was particularly fortunate to find a job working for an audiologist. As a receptionist, my hearing loss became a major issue when answering phones. My employer treated employees like family and he gently nudged me to try different types of amplification. This time, I was mentally ready and determined not to let this lack of ability become a disability.

I went on to earn my Master's degree and have worked and played with children for more than 26 years in public education while raising 3 beautiful daughters. Armed with fond memories of my mother and grandmother, I am sure my girls have grumbled at times when I "encouraged" them to do for themselves what they were capable of doing, or refused to let them take the easy way out. My experience with all of the things that helped me communicate enabled me to teach students with autism and language or learning delays to make sense of nonverbal cues and lead lives that empower them to be more social through meaningful relationships. I am proud of my family and mentors; I hope my mom is proud of my meaningful life.

CHAPTER 1

WORDS, THE 7%

Albert Mehrabian, a pioneer in the field of nonverbal communication, is usually credited with saying it best; communication is a 100% of "something." Through decades of research, he found that less than 10% (that's the 7 of the 7/38/55 rule) of how we communicate comes from the words we speak. Really? Appears so. That is to not say that words are not important, because they are vital for discussions, negotiations, and relationship building; but, we must also understand that our words are not our primary mechanism for communication. For example, a baby's relentless screaming without uttering a single word quickly gets our attention; flailing arms with sweaty skin and bulging eyes glaring in our direction clearly communicates our manager's stress level. And, let us not forget those teary eyes and downward drawn mouth facial muscles inches from our face from a distressed loved one. These are prime examples of the power of the non-verbal.

As an early career middle school Language Arts teacher, I am the first one to value word choice, sentence structure, punctuation, and good grammar; however, I deeply appreciate the significance of the 90%+ of how we communicate beyond the spoken or written word. Nothing can be more irksome than the misuse of "too, two, and to" in a company letter. Or, perhaps, the slaughtered application of "their, there, and they're" typed from a colleague, and emailed to dozens of people around the office. And, to drive this point to an extreme, do you, a rising star or currently brilliant one, want your male peers to consider you the "office girl" - while they remain the "company men?" For the men who consistently introduce us as colleagues, team members, and equals, Bravo!

As we plunge into the formalities of language, research has identified specific mechanisms, or registers, which we use to speak with other people. I had the pleasure many years ago of participating in Dr. Ruby Payne's Framework of Poverty training program and was hooked. The information linked to language structure, working with sensitive populations, and being effective for building relationships was right up my alley. Take a spin as we discuss language registers and how we use these frames to drive our word choices.

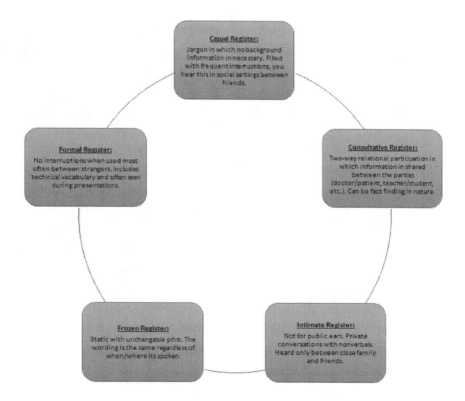

Casual Register:
Jargon in which no background information in necessary. Filled with frequent interruptions, you hear this in social settings between friends.

Consultative Register:
Two-way relational participation in which information in shared between the parties (doctor/patient, teacher/student, etc.). Can be fact finding in nature.

Intimate Register:
Not for public ears. Private conversations with nonverbals. Heard only between close family and friends.

Frozen Register:
Static with unchangable print. The wording is the same regardless of when/where its spoken.

Formal Register:
No interruptions when used most often between strangers. Includes technical vacabulary and often seen during presentations.

Casual Register is as its name infers. We are usually comfortable with this register among our friends and informal relationships. Word choices include slang, generic sentence structure, and the words drive home our intentions with little effort. As you pass by a group of friends, or overhear a friendly and lively conversation, most likely you are witnessing Casual Register. We don't mind interrupting and are rarely concerned with making a good impression. We're equals here.

A conversation, in which we hear advice, expert input, and the like, is operating within a **Consultative Register**. The use of titles, Dr., Mrs., Sir, and so forth, clearly indicate that this register drives the word choice and the intention of the communication. I go so far as to suggest that this book is consultative in nature. A little advice and a mound of expert research, topped with drizzles of experience, are primary ingredients for this book. I also deduce this register drives the work I do and the passions within me as a consultant, colleague, friend, and most importantly, mom. Never at a loss for words or without at least a smidgen of advice, this is what the "theys" of the world say about yours truly. Perhaps you are the same; while ever so slightly nodding your head up and down in agreement while reading this.

Formal Register, on the other hand, requires us to skip the slang and operate using complete sentences with explicit word choices of a higher mental operational platform. Contractions, poor grammar, and jumbled sentence structure are overtly absent from this language. For both the written word and spoken word, formal language is usually the standard at the professional workplace. A smart professional either: 1. Knows and operates from this, or 2. Is now aware of this and will start Monday armed with a shift in the delivery of information through powerful and purposed speech and text to drive her message.

From the most acceptable work-related register, we jump now to the dark side. **Intimate Language.** You can guess based on name alone that this register refers to words communicated between lovers or those involved in ultra-personal, and, at times, sexual relationships. We, as particularly savvy and perceptive women, quickly identify this with this register; often through inappropriate word choices, sexual jokes, and conversations that make most of us blush or cringe. I offer my sage advice to avoid or limit this type of communication, especially in the workplace. A little off-the-record salty conversation with a close friend may be acceptable, but for the most part, steer clear of being known as the Director of Sexual Anything. Behind your back, little good can come of engaging with this type of communication.

Finally, **Frozen Register** is one we have practiced since childhood. Remember *Twinkle, Twinkle, Little Star* or *Patty Cake, Patty Cake*? How about proudly belting out *God Bless America* at your last Memorial Day picnic? I easily can recall and recite the Lord's Prayer as it was a part of my parochial elementary school routine. "Frozen" in time regardless of trends, audiences, and content, we have operated from this register a long time. For example, the *Pledge of Allegiance* and specific Bible verses remain constant regardless of geography, culture, or social environments. You were grateful for this register if you changed schools often and wanted to fit in during the morning routine as the new kid. Can you imagine the verses of The Pledge of Allegiance edited based on whim or geography; or an edited oath making us question its lawfulness in a courtroom?

As you grow and develop yourself as a professional, remember that you are the Board Chair, not the Board Chair<u>man</u>, and will move mountains! While this is not a book about gender disparities, gross injustices, and inequalities, recognize that gender dynamics are a part of how we verbally and non-verbally communicate every day. Therefore, continue to invest in the development of your language, enrich your vocabulary (perhaps through a "word a day" app on your phone), value the meaning of your choice of words, and master the spoken and written word. But, moreover, invest in the influential language of our bodies in that this powerful way of communicating could and should be part of the 100% you!

foul language

swearing

4-letter word

cussing

dirty word

no-no

swearing

blasphemy

profanity

heresy

irreverence

obscenity

expletive

naughty word

Speaking of powerful ways we communicate, I want to [bleep] the [bleep] regarding his [bleep] every time we work on a [beeping] project. I didn't need to actually write the swear words because you know the power of inference. Some people, though, believe that it is acceptable to bring their personal mouths and word choices to the professional work setting. We know these foul-mouthed people because they leave a seared imprint on our brains with their colorful language and, for the most part, it's a negative one. Without much consideration of who's within earshot, these types of people drop the F-bomb like ace fighter pilots, or the B-word without a single hesitation.

Now, I'll be the first to admit that I can have a rather saucy tongue in selective situations, but I guarantee you that I am mindful to the ears in the room, my physical environment, the situation at hand, and mores of other people within earshot. This type of communication is best reserved for dialogue off the grid and with little opportunity for repercussions. The last thing any of us would want is to be passed over for a promotion, or worse, because our mouths explode with shards of vulgarity.

With more than one million words in the English language from which to choose, many people opt for swear words to enhance their stories; and, these people tend to have specific favorites. You know. The F-bomb. The S-word. And, sadly, the B-word that we, as women, are bombarded with in far too many situations and from certain individuals in our lives. It's practically the go-to word/term/descriptor when something isn't just right. Books are titled it. Women drop it on other women. It's a noun, a verb, and a direct object. At its core meaning, though, it does not help women thrive in our vast landscape of social contexts, emotional deposits, and wealth of words. Not to say that it doesn't have its place as a classic descriptor for those ultra-irritating people in our lives, but be cautious as to when and how you opt to use this ear-catching word.

To humor myself, and perhaps you, I searched for synonyms to arm us with selective B-word alternatives which convey our message while not intentionally or blatantly interjecting the dreaded B-word. I offer you 3 Ferris wheels of options based on bitch as a noun, verb, and direct object.

That _____ took my parking space.

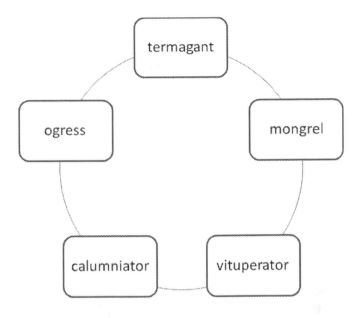

Pat's _____ got on my last nerve.

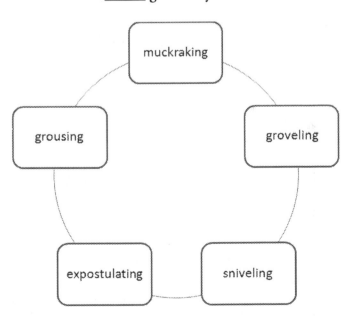

For example: My neighbor's friend is such a _____.

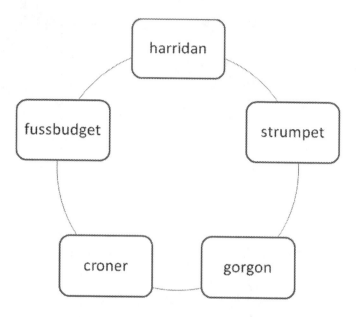

We agree that the definition of communication means the sharing or exchanging of information through social contact. Think about the significance of our words. Recall a person at your work whose language includes an ample supply of profanity, none of which include the Ferris wheels of 15 descriptors anxiously waiting to be included. Does this salty-tongued person make word adjustments when certain people are in the room? Is she loud? Has he taken a brief glance around to see who's within earshot? Does she even seem to care? Now, ask the same of yourself. What's your potty mouth policy at work? Who has the pleasure of hearing you? Are you in Dolby stereo? More importantly, what do the people who hear you think about you, your expansive vocabulary, your message, and your intentions?

Careerbuilder.com and Harris Interactive surveyed more than 5,000 full-time hiring managers and workers from a cross-sector of companies and industries to see if swearing harmed career opportunities and made lasting impressions. Their findings were interesting.

Swearing by Age	Swearing by Gender	Cities Most Likely to Swear	Where You Swear	Bad Impressions
•18-24: 42% •25-34: 51% •35-44: 58% •45-54: 51% •55+: 44%	•54% of men reported swearing at work •47% of women reported swearing at work	•Washington, DC: 62% •Denver: 60% •Chicago: 58% •Los Angeles: 56% •Boston: 56% •Atlanta 54%	•In front of co-workers: 95% •In front of the boss: 51% •In front of senior leaders: 13% •In front of clients: 7%	•81% believe one's professionalism comes into question •71% are concerned with lack of control •68% call it lack of maturity •54% see that person as less intelligent

Did you first look to see how many people in your own age group are likely to cuss at work? Perhaps you saw your workplace city on this list. Were you surprised that both men and women swear at work? Probably not.

Let's focus on the last two topics from the chart above in that they are critical for you, the workplace professional. The data clearly indicates that who you swear in front of matters, and the bad impressions these seemingly simple words, aren't so meaningless. The last thing in the world you want to do is swear in front of someone who, in turn, labels you as unprofessional, out of control, immature, or dumb. However, there's a high probability of this if profanity is a habitual part of your communication, particularly at the workplace.

People make big assumptions about colleagues who commonly incorporate bad (grammar and guttural) language in their daily communication. Remember, first impressions and lasting impressions are just that – impressions. **What imprint do you want to make?** What other words from the one million word pool will you retrieve and make your own? I've included a challenging matching game to get you started on your path to savvy, saucy, and powerful words to season your language and captivate your audience. Feel free to consult with your language app. No judgments.

1. annoy	a. palaver
2. happy	b. farcical
3. bother	c. stellar
4. generous	d. delightful
5. upset	e. gall
6. super	f. substandard
7. ridiculous	g. magnanimous
8. nice	h. perturb
9. bad	i. radiant
10. outstanding	j. superb

How did you do? No doubt, you know thousands of words to incorporate at the workplace to ensure that your professionalism will not be questioned. And, when appropriate, you decide when and where to flavor your message.

I am often asked how someone can expand their vocabulary. Without boring you with the statistical jargon and confidence intervals specific to language development research and childhood experiences hardwired to neuroscience, I found a great online resource from wikiHow for cultivating our word garden. I even created this flashy infographic (with the help of hubspot.com) to capture the essence of their suggestions and ideas for language expansion. You can do the same. The key is constantly and systematically increasing your vocabulary and bank of words. Take that to the bank.

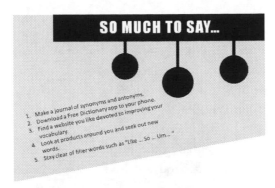

SO MUCH TO SAY...

1. Make a journal of synonyms and antonyms.
2. Download a Free Dictionary app to your phone.
3. Find a website you like devoted to improving your vocabulary.
4. Look at products around you and seek out new words.
5. Stay clear of filler words such as "Like ... So ... Um..."

LEARN NEW WORDS

1. Read voraciously by reading books and magazines every week.
2. Read challenging books as well as the classics.
3. Read about a variety of subjects.
4. Read new and old fiction.
5. Read online sources.
6. Look up any words you do not recognize.
7. Read the dictionary ... and the thesaurus.

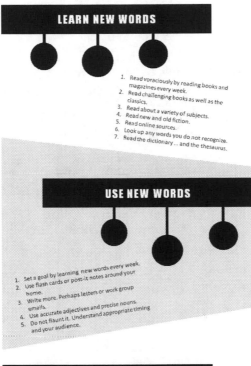

USE NEW WORDS

1. Set a goal by learning new words every week.
2. Use flash cards or post-it notes around your home.
3. Write more. Perhaps letters or work group emails.
4. Use accurate adjectives and precise nouns.
5. Do not flaunt it. Understand appropriate timing and your audience.

BUILD YOUR VOCABULARY

1. Sign up for an online "Word of the Day" email.
2. Do word puzzles and play word games. Scrabble anyone?
3. Learn a little Latin. It's not dead.

Remember, you are a lifelong learner. Invest in yourself!

There is a lot of research on language development and our early childhood experiences. Some people have asked me how I have accrued a hearty vocabulary. To be honest, I grew up around people with plenty to say and expectations through the roof. I was also fortunate to attend an all-girls Catholic high school with unwavering academic and social expectations. Follow this with an unforgettable college experience and the bar was set - and quite the high bar, I might add. You, too, have bars to set and records to break.

I recall my first college English class, at the ripe age of eighteen, in which my first paper submission received a big, fat F. Yes, the F-word; circled in red ink for the world (ok, the half awake class) to see. Talk about a reality check and a new experience for yours truly. By the time the quarter ended, I was never so grateful for that beautifully arched C circled in dazzling red ink. I had improved. I had learned and, often, was humbled for what I did not know. This was the start for many valuable lessons shaping my early adulthood.

So, fear not my fellow communicators and eager minds, I do empathize with the complexity of words and how they are judged. The development of our own language, speaking proficiency, and use of words is relentless. I share this with you to help you understand why you may question your own experience with words or, at times, get frustrated in that your vocabulary isn't ripe with 'big words.' For that, I suggest you grasp a strong hold of the spoken word, use online tools available with just one click, and invest the energy to master and lead with communication building blocks.

As you continue to strengthen your tone, voice, and talents, remember, the written word carries similar weight in both application and judgment. Nothing can be more irksome than to receive an email with misspelled words and poorly timed slang. Or, a teacher's welcome back to school letter highlighting his ignorance on the correct use of "you're child" or "your child" and promptly accentuated with the wrong "too, to, or two." What school did they attend and, more significantly, how many years of English 101 did they sleep through?

If you are not a strong writer and rarely jump at the chance to write the company's holiday letter or weekly press releases, that is perfectly acceptable.

It's A.O.K. No one said you had to be the office wordsmith or keeper of 'all things grammatically correct.' However, there is an expectation in the workplace that the application of common, correct grammar, as part of the English language, be used in both written and spoken communiqué.

Today's workplace requires, to some degree, mastery of text and print. Emails, memos, text messages, and documents besiege us and beg for us to respond. Remember, at any given moment, we may be required to answer an email from a complete stranger who, in turn, will judge us on how and what we write regardless of content. Computer coding gurus, keenly aware of this important fact, have even created a 'check spelling' prompt in that we avoid such a blunder and opportunity to make a bad impression. One little click may make all the difference. Safety first, people. Now hit 'Send.'

Yes, we all make mistakes. To err is human. Or is it, to error is human? In any case, being conscientious of what you write and how you write it is important. It is a part of our message and branding; people make assumptions about how we communicate. They also make assumptions in today's market about the use of social media at the workplace. Is email OK and can I use the same one for both personal and professional transactions? Can I set-up my Facebook account on behalf of the company? Why is YouTube blocked in my building? Why on earth doesn't my boss have a LinkedIn account? Who isn't on Snapchat?

The catalog of questions exceed the time workplace policy-making departments have as they work feverishly to answer questions specific to the expectations of reply, reply all, forward, and friend requests. Social media has its place and is a phenomenal tool for enhancing our message, as long as we remember that we work with humans who lead, follow, and behave quite differently than the text images we insert on social sources.

Case in point. Data was collected on individuals representing a wide variety of US companies, nonprofits, and smaller entities from a Fortune 500 and other well-known databases. More than 4,700 organizations were identified and a total of 461 completed surveys were analyzed. Participants also represented a wide spectrum; including, 54% women, 45% with a Master's degree, 41% making more than $100,000 per year and, on average, with at least 15 years of professional experience in communication. This group of heavy hitters, with decades of cumulative experience and education, offered a wealth of information regarding workplace communication targeting social media, leadership, and behaviors.

The core of the study highlighted three basic points:

1. Social media and leadership behaviors are linked;

2. The type of organization, years of managerial experience, and organizational type significantly impacted social media use; and

3. The use of social media at work was predicated on the communication professional's strategic vision regarding social media.

That last point is an important one. There's a high likelihood that the communication specialist and leadership person or team at your workplace are driving social media decisions, perceptions, hidden-rule usage, and policies. Be astute to know these people and watch them. Do they live on social media and promote posts on behalf of the company? Does the company softball game team photo and after party celebration end up on the cover of a social media post from a colleague? If so, I bet you first stared at the photo to see how you looked.

When you look around, who else is on their phone or do people hide out in the restroom to make calls? We bring our own philosophy and practices about social media to the workplace. Confirm that your values, personal agendas, and behaviors do not interfere with workplace expectations. What is the marketing and advertising budget for your place of business? From printed policies to hidden expectations, each business has an acceptable culture for this type of communication at work.

Ideas to Consider:

1. While vulgar language adds spice to conversations, be cognizant of your audience and learn "colorful language" to express yourself beyond cuss words.

2. How do you really know you're a good communicator?

3. Analyze your written style and word choice by mastering letter, email, and print materials in that your message is branded per your intentions.

4. It's not how much you say (conversation time consumption and incessant talking); but, rather how you select narratives to express how you feel and want to be received by others.

5. Recognize that our emotions and behaviors filter through our words as part of our body language. High emotional intelligence requires a keen understanding of the power of our words.

Take-Away:

Enrich your spoken vocabulary through selective word choice, conversation starters, and articulation. Monitor your social media reputation.

CARBON INTO DIAMONDS	
Reflections ... *What I gleaned from* *this chapter*	Personal Action Plan ... *What I plan to do with* *this new knowledge*

IDIOM EPISODE #1

Mr. Hales believes Ken will be the perfect fit for the job. He asks Liz to step and help with Ken's transition though she's been on the assignment for the last three months.

Sage Story

Let Your Life Speak by Lesley Stiles Scearce

"Resist the urge to become what you think a CEO of United Way should be like, and be you."

Those were the words written to me by a long standing leader in our community when I took on a new role as President / CEO of our area United Way. As the youngest person to serve in this capacity, I have to admit, I wondered what the many expectations would be from the thousands of stakeholders invested in this mission work. Would I live up to them? Is that even possible?

I will never forget the first opportunity to make good on this piece of advice.

I had a candid, casual lunch with a reporter who wanted to "get to know the new CEO." Over fried chicken salads, we talked about our families and what mattered most to us in life. I spoke from the heart about my passions, strengths and candidly, my weaknesses. I shared my leadership tenants about humility and learning through trials and mistakes. I discussed the people who invested in me over the years and told stories about my hardest moments.

The next week the interview appeared in a highly distributed magazine with me on the cover. Our conversation was printed word for word. No edits. Unscripted. Poor grammar. No sound bites. Painstakingly real.

I panicked.

Surely our 75 board members and 22,000 donors need to see a glossy, put together interview with perfectly placed words of wisdom and wit (at least on my first public interview!). I mean, I speak publicly for a living. I can do the perfectly scripted thing. My insecurity kicked in and I spent hours chastising myself for not being more professional, for not being more perfect.

Then I remembered the very words about leadership that I shared with the reporter. I firmly believe that ego is rooted in insecurity and that confidence is rooted in humility. I took my own advice and settled into accepting any outcome that came as a result of this article.

Amazingly, that Sunday in our local newspaper, the same reporter wrote an article about an unnamed, new young leader (that would be me, folks) who taught him that wisdom comes from being humble and self aware. I couldn't believe it. Not only did he say that our conversation had a profound impact on him, but I received dozens of emails from strangers saying they would lead and work differently as a result. One young woman shared that the piece gave her permission to be more honest in her work and her life. Our own staff said it set the stage for building a culture of authenticity.

Will I be more cognizant or prepared in future professional settings? Sure. But, will I wallow in my future failures? No. I will continue to learn and lead with humility and confidence.

The goal in life is not perfection. The goal in life is growing.

So, ladies let your life speak. Fill in the blank with me: Resist the urge to become what you think a (_____) should be like, and be you.

CHAPTER 2

TONE AND VOICE, THE 38%

Don't use that tone with me! Watch what you say! The list goes on and on as to what people say to us and how we hear it. We constantly have to check our tone of voice as we engage with peers, friends, and supervisors. We need to grasp what the research says about almost 40% of how we communicate. Surely, mastery of this would give us the edge, both professionally and personally. One of America's most famous psychologists of all time, B.F. Skinner, even wrote a book identifying and suggesting more than 300 possible research topics about verbal behaviors, humans, and the topic of language. Nothing else; just a list of suggestions. To say that the tone of our voice is powerful would be an understatement. We "hear" what people are saying in many ways. From a sigh to a whisper, the command of our voice is clear and often in our control.

Based in science and behavior, research confirms that a few of our tonal and voice elements are a part of our physiology; whereas, some are well within our control and worthy of learning. Let's examine these unique communication elements of our voice to better understand ourselves. Intentional practicing these subchannel specifics will strengthen us.

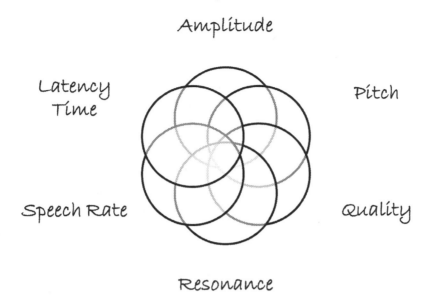

Amplitude

Latency Time

Pitch

Speech Rate

Quality

Resonance

Amplitude

Sometimes people are loud and we wish they had an 'off' switch. To better understand how to work with the 'booming speakers' in the office, park, or movie theater, first consider your own volume. How deafening are you? Is your whispering far, far from a whisper? Do cubicle walls and background noises interfere with your conversations and compete with your air space? Just as we fancy a certain volume on our personal ear buds, we prefer a particular level when speaking with other people. We must also consider the degree of loudness as part of our physical body. Bigger people usually have larger vocal chords, lungs, and air flow. They may just be louder as a person. How amped is your vocal stereo?

Pitch

While we rarely consider the rate that our vocal folds vibrate as we speak, variations in vibration rates are counted, analyzed, and assigned pitch values. Experts spend insurmountable energy to understand this element of speech and their findings are intriguing. The pitch of our voice is tied to the physical size of our folds, their length and thickness, and our hormones; in particular, testosterone. Meaning, we are born with a pitch structure that, through growth stages, change. When someone's pitch produces a low frequency, their folds are thicker and longer, as heard by most adult men. As a side note, the research suggests that women are usually attracted to men with lower pitches at a basic human, mating-potential level.

Pitch has also been extensively studied in which higher pitches, produced by women, are judged by men as "more attractive, more feminine, younger, and more desirable as marriage partners." Really? Apparently so, says the literature. Lest we be offended; focus on the part of pitch which may influence perceptions and, in particular, leadership roles. It has been strongly suggested that, due to the higher nature of a woman's natural voice, leadership roles may favor deeper pitched men. In one study, participants were asked to judge pitch-manipulated recordings of past presidents' voices. Recordings of lower pitched voices were found to have "greater integrity and physical prowess" compared to the higher pitched voices.

The research also confirms that the pitch of our voice is tied to emotion and, often, elevates when emotions kick in. For that reason, we'd be wise to gather our emotions and check how our inner feelings emerge through our voice, even though no words are uttered. I remember a friend telling me a clever story about pitch in that the "higher the pitch, the more trash they've been talking about you!" After hearing this trinket of wisdom, I began to listen to others' pitches when under stress, or with certain people. Let me say that there is, indeed, a connection between our tone of voice and how we engage with others who evoke emotion from us. So, basically, without thinking, your tone may give way to your true feelings if left unchecked.

As to not get any deeper on the subject of pitch and our nonverbal communication at this point, let's agree that this part of our tone of voice is important. It impacts both our communication and perceptions by others. Are you pitch perfect?

Quality

Also referred to sound quality, tone, timbre, and tonality, this part of our nonverbal communication is frequently associated with our emotional state. An interesting body of work cross-analyzed whispering, breathing, harshness, creakiness, and tension with eight different types of emotions. They found that a strong connection between the subtle qualities of our voice can evoke (or provoke) distinct emotions from within us. From a strong reaction to a mild response from our listeners, know that we make memorable connections with other people that impact moods and emotions. We may not consciously adjust the sound quality of our voice, but we clearly remember harsh parental warnings to "Watch your tone with me!" Mom may have been on to something with those five little scary words.

Resonance

From the Latin "to resound or echo," we associate people and feelings because this part of our voice tugs at our emotions. Think of Morgan Freeman's voice as God. Or, how we know when Cher's on stage. At its core, this quality-related voice element helps us make deep and sustaining connections between people, meanings, and time. For example, great storytellers are masters of visual and auditory impressions as they help us see, feel, and remember what we hear. Memorable radio personalities flood the airways because their voices come to life as we tune in with our auditory senses. Who doesn't adore a public figure or popular speaker because of their ability to connect with their audience, evoke emotion, and make their point? Their echoing, literally and figuratively, gets inside our heads.

Now, picture someone on your "I do not like" list who said something to you or about you. Just one, please. Why did you pick that particular name? Did he say something to you offensive or sensitive? Did she plant a seed of doubt or insecurity in your ear? For what rationale thought, beyond his spoken words, did he make your list? Odds are it was the way this not-so-wonderful person made you feel. All the subtle echoing hurt and, in turn, solicited a reaction from you. While the reaction may have first been anger, at the end of the day, Ms. Meanie-Weenie hurt your feelings. She toyed with your emotions. A lasting impression based on words, and backed up by a parade of nonverbal cues, ignited a firestorm of feelings from you. Add a little time to filter or process, and tah-dah, they resonated with you.

Shift this information to the workplace. On a daily basis, we express ourselves, transmit information, make impressions, absorb information, and evoke both critical and emotional responses. That can make for a long day and we haven't even checked our email, Facebook, or Instagram!

Think, before you speak, how you want to intentionally communicate. Consider the implications of our deliberate voice, volume, and pitch before we act or react with our listener. Remember, we can harness our tone of voice and self-regulate which, in turn, will reduce the opportunity for some meanie-weenie to think, or dare, utter, "Put a muzzle on it." Contemplate the echo you produce at work. Hello? Hello? Can you hear me?

Speech Rate

Speaking of muzzles, ever find yourself in the company of the Company Chatterbox? If you could, would you grab a stopwatch and literally count every word that the person is speaking in a single minute (all while you're lacing up your running shoes and planning your escape)? Rest assured, researchers do count those chatters and, in fact, each of us speaks at a different rate per minute. You know these types of people, from one extreme to the other. Some never zip it. Others rarely open it. This part of our voice is quickly judged by others and, all too often, dumped in the negative perception bucket. It's a rather full bucket.

Speech rate data is attention-grabbing and unique to cultures, delivery of information, and, of course, listeners' retention rates. A group of researchers studied the word count in task-oriented conversations based on a myriad of factors: age and role of the speakers, relationship between the speakers, difficulty of the topic, and gender. They found that the 'higher role' speaker spoke over twice as many words compared to the lower labor position.

The data also found variations in word counts between the age of speakers (young, middle, and older), as well as a shift based on the nature or topic of the conversation.

Guess what? They also found no difference in "the number of words uttered by men vs. women." There it is, in print, by the experts. No difference! And, for my blissfully married readers, the experts also found "no difference" in the word counts between married couples vs. strangers. Take that to the bank on your next wordy conversation with Mr. or Mrs. Matrimony if accused of being relentlessly talkative!

Note, though, that this morsel of knowledge does not give us license to incessantly chat-it-up at work and evoke our free flowing speech motor-mouths. How much we do talk does matter in the average, daily, important discussions, conversations, presentations, and speeches. Our ears are constantly in the 'on' position and, more than we realize, people are pressing the stopwatch. I would like to believe that time is on my side with my ability to self-regulate my jaw, mouth, throat, larynx, and what comes from within. What is your self-regulatory capacity?

The research on this subject of talk time is impressive and important for us, particularly at work where 'time is money' and 'we never have enough of either' (not that I necessarily agree with either of those popular idioms). One study confirmed that the rate of our speech is rooted in our speaking style and the scenario at hand. That makes sense. Another study dove deeper to help us understand what happens when we speak too many words per minute. I've provided some key bullet points as to avoid the bullets you might receive from fed up co-workers who may not appreciate your 1,000 word count per minute talent:

- The "optimal rate" we process information is between 170 and 190 words per minute.

- If we talk less than 170 words per minute, then our listener cannot pay attention. We are less dynamic, and they zone out. You know, the potential for the eye glaze to nowhere look.

- If we talk more than 190 words per minute, our listener will find us hard to follow, especially if we are talking about complex stuff. Again, the image of a deer in the headlights.

- If we talk more than 210 words per minute, our listener will suffer and, most likely, abandon the conversation. Run, Forest, Run.

Hence, when we have to talk about multifarious ideas or issues plaguing us and driving our deadlines, slow down, and seek comprehension. Confirm understanding beyond the bobble-head nods and donut-glazed eyes. Whereas, if we are chattering about normal, everyday ideas and issues, speed up and carry on. Remember, success comes from the listener's point of view, not our own stopwatch. You can count on it.

designed by freepik.com

Latency Time

A point to consider. I mention that this next part of our tone of voice is usually linked with geography, culture, childhood, and our emotions. Wow. That sounds much worse than 'a point to consider' after I typed it. While its scientific term is latency speech patterns, we know this is as the "talk-wait-talk" time factor. You know, it's when someone says something and then there is this gap or space in time - then the other person says something. Let's talk about the gap and its strong connection to location and situation.

Latency, or wait time, can make a significant difference on how our message is heard. When two people talk, each usually has something to say and drags in a host of emotions to deliver the message. There's ample opportunity for the message to get lost, misinterpreted, or trigger emotions. For example, watch and listen to two people excited about something. Do their words fly back and forth quicker than a ping pong competition and there is literally zero wait time between the two? No one's coming up for air. Or, does one person speak and then the other wait, patiently, pause, and then respond? We see this activity and also engage in this practice almost every time we are talking with someone.

Consider a work scenario and think about two people having a conversation. Now, only consider the latency periods between the two voices. You can almost count the space. One second? Two seconds? Or, do you hear one voice melting into the other voice? This intriguing part of how we speak impacts our listener. You know this because you have experienced it - usually with a negative reaction. Remember that time you wanted to tell someone something super important? When you talked and then stopped, they immediately jumped in and, as you recall, practically steamrolled over you. You waited patiently and then started again with your really super important story. Again, they killed the space between your voice and their voice. They jumped in. They took over. You quickly concluded that they just did not care about your really super important story. Or, they're just rude.

Let's switch the latency time the other way and try again. You have a really incredibly innovative idea you've been slaving over all weekend,

27

and it's now the topic of discussion between someone at work and you. You start with your most brilliant, or not so brilliant, sentence and look anxiously into your listener's eyes for their feedback. Cricket. Cricket. Cricket. (Cricket = 1 second, unless it's going poorly, then Cricket = 1 minute). You immediately think, maybe they weren't listening. Should I say it again? Are they really thinking it over before they speak? What is that worthy of such consideration? Your crazy, quick, rationale brain concludes with a clever question like, "Did you hear me?"

You understand the latency part of speech and how our emotions quickly, and usually without thinking, get involved. Our critical brains try to make sense of the spoken and, more importantly, unspoken spaces as we communicate with other people. Regardless of status, topic at hand, or critical lessons to be learned, we should consider how we respond to cricket time and receive it. While we typically could care less about plowing over our close friends' sentences, this is not the case at work.

As an astute professional, take the time to consider the time you start to speak after someone stops talking. Remember, your body, particularly your face, is fully "talking" - though your words are constrained. Be intentional about what you see, what you hear, and how you are conducting yourself. That's the whole business of active listening that we will address later in Chapter 3.

Other factors to consider are geography and culture. In certain regions of our country, it is considered rude to wipe-out the latency space when engaged in conversation. If violated, the talk-wait-talk rule is mentally challenged and the message received includes thoughts of inconsideration or lack of manners. Whereas, others have no problem with rapid fire feedback between two people having a lively discussion. It saves time. I know what you're thinking anyway. I'm ready to respond. I'm all in. **Therefore, be intentional and aware of your surroundings.**

Quickly consider others' speaking styles and their wait times when you speak with them. If you want to build trust and receive an A+, then match their wait times. You will be perceived as considerate, thoughtful, and worthy of a second conversation. Use your nodding, leaning in, and supportive facial nonverbals to show your listener that you hear them. In the words of Shakespeare, "To be or not to be." In the words of Dr. Donna Van Natten, "To pause, or not to pause." <u>That</u> is the question.

Slip of The Tongue

Finally, I address a part of our communication which, for many, may seem trivial. A misspeak. A slip up. An error in speech that, according to Wikipedia psycholinguistic experts, is defined as "verbal errors that have since been titled 'Freudian slips.' Those errors in speech that are said to occur due to the interference of an unconscious wish, need, or thought." Freudian aside, this highly complex process is extremely difficult to thoroughly understand. It involves intricate mental mechanisms; let alone, trying to understand the brain. But the research on this piece on how we communicate is captivating and associated with animal behaviors in countless studies. Let's bring out the animal in us for a moment, shall we?

From sign language to slips of the tongue, these mistakes offer a glimpse into our brains and how we experience language. As you probably can guess - words that we don't use often are subject to fewer mishaps; whereas, common words like cat and bat frequently used in conversations, are processed differently in our brain process language coding center.

By William H. Calvin, PhD - Own work, CC BY-SA 4.0,
https://commons.wikimedia.org/w/index.php?curid=49108227

Kanzi, currently 35 years old and residing in the great state of Iowa, helped researchers with how we code language by responding to instructions and descriptions in English. Using lexigrams on a keyboard, Kanzi was successful 12,157 times compared to 1,497 recorded errors. For you overachiever academics, that's an 89% success rate, a B+ circled in bright red ink; and she's an endangered dwarf chimpanzee great ape. A bonobo species, not only is she smart, but you'll notice her by her "relatively long legs, pink lips, dark face, and tall-tuft, with parted long hair on her head." Thank you wikipedia.com for this charming description.

Back to slips in our speech. You might appreciate this opportunity to expand your vocabulary. I'll give you a multiple choice question and you pick the correct answer: What do we call that accidental mishap in speech where we mix up the initial sounds of two words used in a sentence? Here is an example; "wave the sails" comes out like "save the whales." Your choices: a) spoonerism; b) synonym; c) conjunction; d) onomatopoeia. As to not distract you with testing and trivia, the answer is found at the end of the chapter. This is just one example of how we slip in speech. Carry on.

Why do we say what appears to be such simple mistakes in how we speak? I wish the answer was simple. Actually, when this happens, the act of "pause and correct" will suffice. Pause to give yourself a mental re-group, and then say the correct phrase. We know there is a connection between comprehension and nonverbal support activities, but there is no definitive answer as to why we make mistakes in speech. Perhaps Freud has the answer, "There are no mistakes." Thanks, Sigmund.

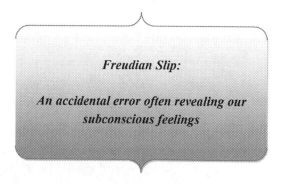

Freudian Slip:

An accidental error often revealing our subconscious feelings

As we reflect on the pieces of this chapter and our tone of voice, a gleaning of the various parts of our tone of voice might start us on our way to concluding this chapter. My 'glean clean' questions for you, the consummate professional, include:

- How loud are you in the workplace?

- When someone triggers an emotional response from you, do you get rather pitchy?

- What might "watching your own tone" look, feel, and sound like?

- How will you assess if you're talking too much?

- Do you always look like you are actively listening to your colleague and monitor your own use of cricket time?

- Where might you decide to engage with your tone of voice given certain situations, all the while respecting unique cultural differences?

- How often do you use your personal spell-check and mental voice-check during opportunities to communicate?

- When a mental slip occurs, how will you "pause and correct?"

Ideas to Consider:

1. Conduct a personal sound check.

2. Conduct an office sound check. What background noises are static, like the air conditioner and elevator music? If you have a cubicle office, background sounds are amplified. Hence, check your volume – the radio, the phone, the mouth.

3. Watch how other people interact and study how they use latency times to enhance their messages. Incorporate unspoken spaces to

elevate your ideas. In the words of Susan Scott, perhaps "let silence do the heavy lifting."

4. Understand and appreciate that when in Rome, do as the Romans do. If you need to slow down your rate of speech for better comprehension, don't balk, simply do it. If the situation warrants a time crunch and is filled with a basket of emotional colleagues, be the mast rather than the wave.

5. Consider learning the nuances that make speech rich and practice decreasing your own error rates. Inject vibrant language when it's your turn to speak; not to demonstrate how smart you are and need for others to know. But, for helping your listeners remember what you said.

6. The answer: a.

Take-Away:

A personal sound check may be in order. People hear almost all of your sounds and sighs. These sounds speak loudly about your inner feelings and thoughts, and impact your outward behaviors.

CARBON INTO DIAMONDS	
Reflections ... *What I gleaned from this chapter*	Personal Action Plan ... *What I plan to do with this new knowledge*

The team hesitantly decides Ms. Hatfield will lead the project. Eager to dive in, she gathers her team for a brainstorming session. You bring your thoughts to the meeting; so do others.

designed by freepik.com

Sage Story

The Elephant and the Donkey by Sylvia Skrel

Both verbal and non-verbal communication is essential in our lives. It was especially important for me as a public official. I have been told that I am a "people person." I have concluded that it is because I talk "to" people and not "at" them.

When I was elected to the Michigan House of Representatives in 1980, I was keenly aware that 'complete' communications played a very distinct and important role for me.

The Michigan Legislature consisted of 38 Senators and 110 Representatives. At the time, there were no female Senators and only 15 female Representatives. Of the 15 female Representatives, 10 were Democrats and 5 were Republican. I was 1 of the 5 Republicans. I knew I had to communicate with all my colleagues by understanding and talking with, not at, them to garnish their support. It was a constant challenge! When I spoke on the House floor to oppose or support a bill or amendment, I spoke briefly and to the point; carefully choosing my words. My tone and inflections were important to ensure I didn't sound as if I was reading a script. I knew I succeeded because I received support from the Black Caucus, the Polish Caucus, the Republicans, as well as the Democrats. My verbal and nonverbal communication techniques were working!

Over the years, I spoke to many groups and gave many speeches. One group I spoke to included almost 200 members of the UAW-CIO Union (my district was in the Detroit area). My campaign manager insisted I do this even though the union never endorsed or contributed any funds to Republicans. When I arrived at the Union Hall, the union bosses offered me a chair behind a long table where 5 of them were seated. Understanding the importance of where and how I was seated, I politely refused! Additionally, I preferred to stand when I gave a speech to increase my sense of presence (I am, after all, 5' 4"). This enabled me to be both closer to the audience and eliminated the table barrier between us - giving a feel and reality of 'being with them.'

As I began my speech, I searched the audience for a friendly sign or smile. I found none. Then, an elderly grouchy-looking man, seated in the front row, waved his arms to get my attention because he had a question. I walked over to him, made eye contact, and spoke directly to him. I focused on 'our' conversation. I had to calmly educate him on my position and took time to thoroughly explain my answer. I was careful with what I said and, more importantly, how I said it. Centering on my tone and cadence, I watched his reaction and I knew he understood me because his frown softened as he unfolded his arms. The next day, I was informed that the union would contribute only the minimum amount to my opponent and would not press to defeat me. They felt they could work with me because of what I said and how I spoke to their members. They added, "She was the first person to ever make the old man agitator speechless."

A smaller group I spoke to was a high school class in an effort to get volunteers to help with my campaign. One student asked me what I thought of legalizing marijuana. I decided to add a little humor. I made eye contact with him and asked him if he was offering me a joint. Everyone laughed. I had connected with the class. A little empathy goes a long way!

Ask yourself, in your conversations, do you listen, talk with respect, and make eye contact? Or, do you let our eyes roam, seemingly showing disinterest? A conversation is between you and your audience; be it 1 or 200. It is a give and take. Of course, substance is important. However, the delivery is imperative. Am I talking, engaging, and listening to them? Or, at them? I am gratified that actively communicating with people has contributed to my success over the past 80+ years. This is something I constantly practiced throughout my personal life, my career in public office, and as a lobbyist in Washington, DC.

CHAPTER 3

EMOTIONS + BRAIN + COMMUNICATION = TANGLED TALK

As the science of emotional intelligence gathers speed in today's professional development trainings, we know there is a connection between our critical brain, emotional brain, and how we express this through our nonverbal actions and tone of voice. Dr. Paul Broca's brain research confirms that language is closely tied to a large part of our brain which is linked to speech patterns. This powerful area of our brain allows us to put words in context and helps us understand the *real* meaning of someone's message. This is often the basis for emotional intelligence research and understanding the functions of the brain specific to language and behaviors.

Brain mapping has also helped the average person, myself included, grasp language comprehension by making sense of ambiguous information and our sensitivity to other people. Broca even gets the credit for impressive brain mapping, referred to as Broca's Brain (area), and the new age science helping us understand our hard and soft wiring. In essence, we have hard hiring which enables us to understand what people are "saying" beyond words by comprehending elements of voice and tone.

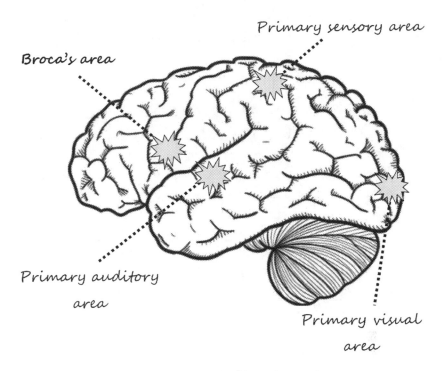

Primary sensory area

Broca's area

Primary auditory area

Primary visual area

designed by freepik.com

As to <u>how</u> we decide to communicate with our brains and emotions leaves us in a powerful or vulnerable position. A bit too brash and brainy and you're labeled a know-it-all. A softy in both behaviors and words, you might be perceived as weak and willing to surrender during an argument. To make things even more complicated, while we may think we lead with our brains and critical thoughts in the workplace or with a colleague, we quickly react with our emotions, question others' words, and toss in a few nonverbal responses. Simultaneously, our brains are silently screaming, "Stop."

Let's start. As women, we do a lot and, for the most part, we are good, really good deliverers. We juggle and focus; scan and hone; speak volumes while silent; and instinctively process massive chunks of miniscule details. That is a busy brain. However, everything comes at a price, especially on the work front where external forces are constantly flooding us as we're mastering new strokes and teaching others to swim. Let's, as women, help others learn to swim the shark infected waters of challenging workplaces. I pledge my commitment to share, guide, and educate my fellow women of all stages and ages about the opportunities we have within to sparkle. Men, you are included, too.

Technically, the female brain and the male brain look and act about the same. However, how these brains are used, nurtured, emotionally fed, and critically engaged differ between men and women. I follow with some entertaining and educational information about the brain and how we, as unique women and men, communicate.

Cool Study #1

With a simple understanding of two areas of our brains and what they control, we begin to understand how women and men differ in tasks, cooperation, skills, and strategies necessary for successful outcomes. The right temporal lobe is responsible for auditory perception like hearing and processing information from others' words. This part helps with memory and is build to capture pictures, faces, directions, and music. Sometimes, it helps with our verbal memory, especially the pitch part. This part is also brings in the personality.

The right inferior prefrontal cortex (aka the inferior frontal gyrus) handles the bulk of language comprehension and syllable information coding. That takes us back to Broca's Brain. Aligning with this study, it's the part the handles "go/no go" tasks, impulse control, and basic risk attitudes. For women, that may suggest that, when paired together for specific tasks, we shine due to our strong right brains with incredible hearing and memory capacities. I know; you don't need a study to affirm that statement! But, let's look at one anyway.

Seven researchers studied the brains of 222 participants using two minute, computer-based tasks and recorded what they say by attaching a ton of wires to each skull and capturing scans. In a series of male (M) and female

(F) combinations, in which they did not include age or ethnicity, they found some significant differences between parts of the brain. I'll now highlight 3 findings and, if you are seeking more, I suggest a subscription to Scientific Report's fNIRS hyperscanning study in the June 2016 issue. Allow me to wear my mind-reader hat: You don't have time for that. Read on.

Three finding summaries in "Donna-speak." First, when one M was matched with either a M (M + M) or with a F (M + F), they saw an increase in behavior performance. In F + F, not the case. Secondly, when F + F completed a task, the researchers noticed significant inter-brain coherence in the right temporal cortex. Whereas, a M + M pairing saw action in the right inferior prefrontal cortex. Thirdly, when the same sexes were paired (F + F or M + M) and asked to complete activities, they captured a connection between task-related inter-brain coherence and cooperative task performance.

Why are there differences in tasks and cooperation based on gender? We always hear about gender equality (or neutrality at work) and statements like, "I work the same regardless of who I'm partnered with for this project." The experts suggest that gender, the biological variable for this study, does, in fact, influence cooperation behavior, cortical activities, inter-brain locations, and the interactions between brain and behavior. When we consider the right and left sides of the brain as well as the temporal or inferior prefrontal regions of the brain, we are different. We think and do, at times, see the world differently and it's even scatter-plotted on paper as proof.

Inferior prefrontal cortex

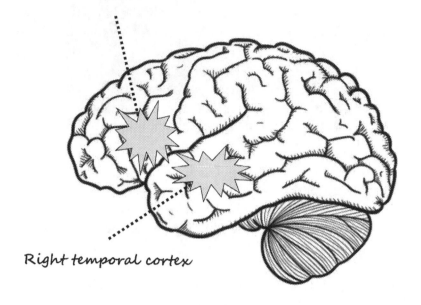

Right temporal cortex

designed by freepik.com

Cool Study #2

Gray matter. White matter. Does it really matter? A California research team studied general intelligence in women and men and, not surprisingly, found no notable differences. However, they did find huge differences specific to white matter and gray matter. Women had more white, men more gray. Both are designed for equal intelligences, so say the experts. Basically, they asked 17 men and 10 women of college age, 25 years on average, to submit themselves to a battery of tests. Participants took IQ and performance tests, and verbal assessments. They then captured images of their brains using MRIs. After crazy analyses, the team calculated the percentage of white and gray matter between the two genders. The details are intense and this is not a book about neuroscience and cognitive brain mapping.

Therefore, we shall explore why gray and white matter may be important for understanding ourselves. A male's brain is about 60% gray brain matter and 40% white matter. A woman's brain is the opposite, 60% white and 40% gray matter. White brain matter connects the gray matter and carries the nerve impulses to get the information there at rapid speed. Now, if we connect that Cool #2 Study with our black and white and gray brains, what does it all mean? Are women capitalizing on that 60% exploding white matter and making connections fast and furious? Are men making the most of their muscles and sensory brain blasts with their gray matter? Could it be a matter of gray and white rather than the classic black and white statements? Perhaps. But remember, just because MRIs capture the percentages of gray and white brain matter, this does not preclude us from asking, "What's the matter?" The determinants are much more intricate and emotionally charged.

Cool Study #3

One final study discusses our brains, gender, and the sensitive topics of depression and sadness. I selected this one because, too often, women do not take care of themselves, each other, and address our own mental well-being. We all know someone who is sad, withdrawn, or blue. Hopefully, we try to connect with her or him. I share this study's key points in that they are also linked to our strong emotions and hormones as women. Conducted in China, 23 male and female patients with various levels of depression were studied. They had seemingly normal work, life, and study patterns. All completed tasks asking them to assess photographs with positive, negative, and neutral images. Their eye movements were tracked and pupil diameter changes were significant based on gender. They also took a horde of tests before the eye tasks with pictures experiment.

For women, pupil sizes changed twice the rate of men, with emotional reactions to the photos. When the photos evoked positive emotions, the pupils changed slightly. When the photo shown elicited a negative emotion, pupil diameters were significantly greater than that of the male group shown the same image. Given the sensitivity of negative images with a group of depressed participants for study, the researchers concluded that female patients had significantly stronger negative emotional experiences linked to the severity of female depression. They also tied estrogen and androgen to the study in that these sex hormones impact levels of stress.

Wow, isn't that possibly depressing for us, as women. Negativity. Hormones. Gender. Stress. We are surrounded by these factors daily and yet, we thrive, with the right support. Let's continue to help each other. **Ensure that no woman is left behind.**

Harvard Business Review (HBR) also provides a wealth of women in the workplace research acknowledging the benefits reaped from investing in women. Allow me to share a few of the good, and the concerning, based on a culmination of studies authored by HBR. For women, take note of the good and the concerning. For men, particularly those with the power to impact workplace change, be conscious of these statistics.

The Study	The Good for Women	The Concerning
High Potential	25% report to the C-suite	33% of men report to the C-suite
Work/Life Balance	60% work after their second child	90% leave because of workplace problems
The Corporate Ladder	325,000 had entry-level positions with major corporations	7,000 made it to the VP, senior VP, or CEO level
Career Confidence	We do get those management and consulting post MBA jobs	We don't believe we will get the jobs in finance, so we don't apply
Parent Bias	Working mothers were recommended for hire	But, offered $11,000 less, on average, than single women
Performance Evaluations	We receive excellent, stellar, and terrific comments more than our male colleagues	But only 6% of these women are mentioned as potential partner material compared to men (15%)

As for our brains and emotions and communication, the triad of unlimited opportunities is boundless. The research is explosive and some topics swirling the scholarly classrooms of our most brilliant focus on areas such as:

Emotions + Faces + Communication
Attachment + Communication + Self-Regulation
Communication + Vocal Expression + Emotions
Brains + Infants + Empathy
Healing + Neuroscience + Emotions

The topics are infinite and I mention a few combinations you may wish to explore for further study. You might pick up a fact or two (million) to share at the next office social. Even a good read on the Polyvagal Theory (see Glossary) might be of interest for some of your curious brains.

designed by 🌐 freepik.com

Two professors of organizational behavior and business penned an article on creating the best workplace on earth. Published in Harvard Business Review, they captured the essence of a thriving workplace, meeting employees' needs, and ensuring the qualities necessary for rewarding work. Both knew that leaders and their organizations must be authentic, or people would not follow. The fact that a company nurtures individual differences will add value and ensure that the company stands for something. The authors identified a series of principles shared by successful and rewarding companies. First, their two universal truths: 1. The best companies clearly know what they do well, and 2. They remain cautious of fads and fashions driving the mainstream corporate world.

As we apply this way of thinking for supporting women and men in the workplace, designing and improving a work environment requires work on both ends, from the establishment and from every individual. That's a challenge; every single person? Really? But, when we nurture individuals, we can be ourselves because the best in us surfaces. Trust is high and we are encouraged to express our differences without fear. A stellar organization values the diversity of its people, including you. I know this may sound altruistic; yet realize, we have choices about where we want to work. If you feel trapped, perhaps you should do something about it. Consider how your employer's values align with your own. **Our values are the seeds of our being.**

As we seek to foster a trusting and open workplace, remember that, "to get at the root cause" of a problem, the "flow of honest information" must exist. That's no easy task. Honesty can sting. Feelings are raw. Ample ego-bruising opportunities exist; and, assaults on our emotional and critical brains tell us to gloss over the hard stuff to avoid potential disasters. That little voice in us screams, "This might hurt me." But, then again, think about the payoff for such risks. Professional and personal growth. Transparency from both the leader and the follower. Opportunities for optimization. Authenticity of self. Where do we begin?

Listen.

And, not just with your two ears, but with your whole person. Active engagement and the process of communicating with another person require that we focus on them and absorb the wealth of information they share with us. From the tone of her voice, to his words, and body behaviors, the polished listener is able to pick-up on the emotional and critical elements of what someone is saying and inferring beyond the words. More often than not, we get so excited to answer a question, make our position known, take a stand, react, or comment that we fail, and I mean miserably fail, to listen to the other person. We all know this, and truthfully, have experienced it from both perspectives. This is where an ounce of honesty may prevent a pound of pain as you grow your career.

How well do you listen? If you were to ask your friends, colleagues, and leaders to rate your active listening skills as part of effective communication, how well would you do? Perhaps, we have two ears and one mouth for a reason. When I spoke with CEOs and those in executive roles, I asked what they felt made them successful. Their overwhelming response is that they listened. They listened to their people. Who would have thought that Ms./Mrs./Mr./Dr. CEO would have said this instead of strategic thinker, executor, risk-taker, and traits traditionally associated with success? That means, perhaps, that listening is a hard and valuable asset imperative for leadership positions.

Research confirms that the art and science of active listening includes verbal and nonverbal communication. One study affirms the powerful part of our nonverbal cues as we ask ourselves,

- ☐ "What kind of listener am I?"

- ☐ "Do I hear only the words?"

- ☐ "Do I listen consistently?"

- ☐ "What do I sense from their body movements as they speak?"

- ☐ "Am I able to pick up their slight tonal and voice parts?"

- ☐ "What is the true meaning of their message beyond the words?"

Just because we <u>hear</u> someone does not mean we are <u>listening</u> to them. Active listening requires authentic engagement with the other person and being present. That's tough to do in an environment filled with noises, demands, emotions, unanswered emails, and a slew of meetings with a thousand voices bombarding the air space. I have created a LISTEN acronym to help illustrate how we may want to incorporate sound active listening techniques.

> **L – Look.** Our culture likes eye contact. Watch her facial and body expressions. The whole body.

> **I – Inquire.** Ask relevant questions without offering advice. Help him help himself. Reflect.

> **S – Situation.** There's a time and place to be an active listener. Be cognizant of the environment.

> **T – Time.** We all share the same amount, but how we value it impacts our listening time.

> **E – Engage.** Remember that, while you're watching him, he's watching you. Be present.

> **N – Navigate.** We all have demands consuming us. Now might be a good time to listen.

Does all of this make your brain spin on overload or squeal with excitement? Listen. Think. Feel. Respond. Don't respond. Reflect. Act. It's a menagerie of opposites, or so it seems, for many aspects of our world and how we operate from within. Know that our brains and hearts have an unbreakable force driving what we say, think, and feel. Own the fact that we, as women, have twice as many emotions as our male counterparts and this revelation explodes and implodes simultaneously.

As we vacillate between presenting ourselves as strong, competent, accomplished, and untouchable professional woman with our feminine, nurturing sides, and emotional outbursts, the balance can feel way too wobbly at times, to say the least. For some, it can feel overwhelming and, in times of stress, our bodies and brains collide. To address this galaxy of internal and external forces, first, may the force be with you (cue *Star Wars* music here). Second, take some time and begin to understand the emotionally intelligent (EI) aspect of yourself. The field of EI is interesting and, not surprisingly, starts with an authentic assessment of self. This EI stuff is tricky, though. Be careful that you don't take a single survey, usually online, to determine your degree or level of EI. Manipulating where you really are and where you think you are can result in two very different scores. The EI process requires numerous reflective and challenging activities and, if you are lucky, feedback from others. This check and balance action means that you will be vulnerable. Scary.

That brings us back to trust. You know, the "circle of trust," famously quoted in the movie, *Meet the Fockers*, that lays the foundation for trust in all relationships. In the arena of trustworthiness, are we willing to let our peers, subordinates, and supervisors rate us? I don't have the answers, but as you slide down the slippery slope of emotional growth while swimming in the professional waters, gauge how you trust the world and are viewed as trustworthy. A requirement for airplane safety, put your mask on first before assisting others. Aren't you glad I didn't say, put your muzzle on first before communicating with others? I thought so.

Ideas to Consider:

1. Talk with your team about a 360 feedback process to dive deep into yourself and how you are perceived by others. Feedback can be hard to stomach; be prepared for hard work to follow.

2. Decide how you want to use your brain when communicating with someone. Do I let my emotions drive my actions or do I embrace my critical brain for solutions without feelings of personal attacks?

3. Learn to listen. Practice it often. Proof of this will be others' responding to you and a reputation of approval will be solicited from office members.

4. If you must, cover your mouth while others are speaking. Literally block the fact that you want to say something. Let your silence be a vehicle of strength and control. Leaders know this. You know this.

Take-Away:

Female and male brains are different. Embrace the variety because both have value in the workplace. The simple necessity for positive leadership: Listen.

CARBON INTO DIAMONDS

Reflections ... *What I gleaned from this chapter*	Personal Action Plan ... *What I plan to do with this new knowledge*

IDIOM EPISODE #3

Ms. Chowell assembles her office staff to assign tasks. The deadline is looming and she's not too happy about what just came down from Corporate.

Sage Story

Scalpel by Michele Hicks

Healthcare, in a hospital setting, is primarily a female dominated field, working alongside male physicians. I have experienced this first-hand as a registered nurse (RN) in the emergency room (ER), intensive care, and operating room (OR). Each setting had unique displays of nonverbal communications. For example, when a patient was brought into the ER via ambulance, healthcare attendants each had a different role that they automatically assumed. I would grab the monitoring items and begin putting them on the patient - like clockwork. The physician started to assess the injuries while listening to the report given by the attendants. The next time, if the physician wasn't there, I received the report. When the attendants left, I had to give my report to the physician. We, nurses, are a wealth of knowledge and influence. As soon as she (it's usually a female) starts to tell the physician (it's usually a male) what she thinks is the problem, he may roll his eyes as if to discredit her depth of knowledge. As long as he is allowed to make the diagnoses, he's in charge. A well run ER depends on all members of the team practicing mutual respect.

Intensive care units, different from an ER, have many other obstacles to overcome to deliver patient care. As an RN, I would admit the patient and develop an individualized care plan based on diagnoses and physician orders. Often times, patients were admitted with one diagnoses and then start to show other signs and symptoms that were not initially present at the time of admission. A trusted RN was present all the time, and made decisions - even when the physician wasn't nearby. I had to communicate, in words and written orders, the vital facts so that physician decisions could be made without necessarily seeing the patient. Few physicians appreciated a 2 AM phone call and this was obvious by the tone on the other end of the call. As a nurse, I had better be right about 1. The patient's pressing needs; and 2. Making that 2 AM call without being spot-on about the patient's condition. Otherwise, a cold-shouldered physician would greet me during morning rounds.

The OR has an entirely different set of rules. In a close physical setting, I, the scrub nurse, assisted the surgeon by handing over tools and watching reactions. As an experienced nurse, I could anticipate what the surgeon required – just at the right time. Novice nurses needed the surgeon to tell them step-by-step. Every surgeon has his or her own sign language.

During one surgery, a medical student was observing our procedure. As she watched, she was amazed at how the surgeon "talked nonstop" to his physician assistant, but never once spoke to me. Yet, the procedure was a success. At the end of the surgery, the med student asked me how I did it. My answer, "It's all in the hands." Confused, I demonstrated the hand signals. Wanting scissors, my surgeon would use his index finger and make a cutting motion. Hemostats were passed with just an open hand. A stitch was a clenched hand - with a turn at the end. These silent actions were performed like clockwork.

What disasters could happen if the little turn at the end of the clenched fist was missed? A wrong instrument placed in the surgeon's hand might be thrown back. Nonverbal communication is essential in the OR. Without being able to see into the wound, I can tell if there is a problem just by the physician's nervousness. We can't see most facial cues due to masks; so I rely on the movements of the physician for clues. The masks hide many nonverbal expressions that we rely on every day. Therefore, expressive eyebrow movements help to understand the real intention. I also receive a message by looking into the eyes.

I once heard a photographer say to a model, "Make your eyes smile." Try covering up your face, but leave just your eyes exposed; see if you can make different expressions with your eyes. This, too, remains an effective method of communication in the OR. Intelligence is confirmed with the quickness of our actions and understanding what the surgeon needs without asking questions.

Regardless of the situation, all share one vital component. Keeping the family informed. Highly sensitized family members can read most nonverbals. My voice is telling them that things are OK, but my face is showing hints of fear and worry. Some physicians are good at hiding their fear when speaking to family members, but afterwards, they come to me, the nurse, for reassurance.

Nursing is a science; and a social skill. We combine all of our knowledge, technical, and social skills into one nonverbal construct to prove that we are a valued team member and caregiver.

CHAPTER 4

NON-VERBALS, THE ALL-IMPORTANT 55%

So now we've reached the heart of how we communicate on a grand scale. It's worth taking some time to explain about how I am going to "talk" body language with you even though I started talking the language on page one. As you progress through topics above the shoulders and below the belt, I will use clinical body terminology; including crotch display, pelvis, and breasts, when necessary. These areas are, in fact, parts of our human body.

As you quickly learned by flipping through the first few pages of this guide, this is about you, your body, how you communicate with it, and what intentional actions enhance or harm you - all sprinkled with heavy doses of humor-dust. As a result, you will be a better communicator. So, thank you in advance for reading beyond the delicate, and at times, culturally offensive, words to reading between the lines and garnishing the nuggets. Our mutual understanding of the 50%+ of how we communicate beyond the spoken word will serve us well.

While this chapter discusses the "whole body," subsequent chapters will dive deeper into detailed body parts and regions. I have provided a not-so-famous alteration of a famous body to illustrate our whole body.

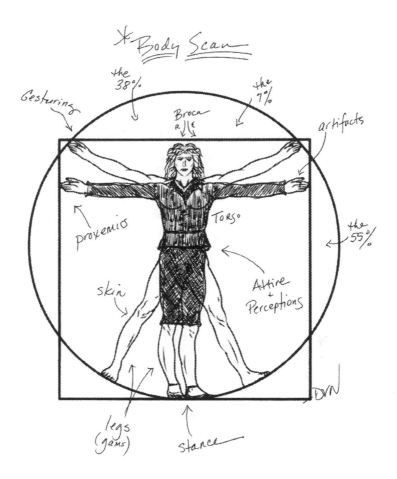

*Body Scan

the 38%
Gesturing
Broca R/L
the 7%
artifacts
proxemics
Torso
the 55%
skin
Attire + Perceptions
legs (gams)
stance
DVN

You know **Da** Vinci *man*. Now you know **Donna Van** Natten *woman* and the power of the woman within each of us! What you see is an overall structure for this book based on physical sections of our bodies. **Chapter 5** will address research and nonverbal behaviors specific to our face, hair, smiles, and all the nuances that make us big workplace communicators beyond our words and tone of voice.

In **Chapter 6**, I give ample time to handshakes because they are that important. We often overlook such a seemingly trivial activity, but I promise, you won't feel the same or practice that wet fish hand clamp again after reading. I also include culturally-driven gestures that people, worldwide, use to emphasize their verbal messages. From a correct hand position to an offensive use of finger formations, gestures are influential for how we communicate.

Heading south, literally, **Chapter 7** examines how we use our feet, legs, hips, and crotch displays to transmit and receive thoughts. We often overlook the subtle messages coming from these areas unless presented overtly for our viewing and, usually, with aggressive or sexual intentions. Ideas for acting and reacting with your nonverbals are included, as well as amusing data from primates paralleling humans. No surprises!

Chapter 8 discusses how imperative it is how we carry ourselves, as women and professionals, at the workplace and outside the work day. From sitting to posing and carrying our carriage, we emit confidence or insecurity with our frame. As a 5'11½" female Avatar, I may know a thing or two about standing tall, literally and figuratively. Plus, for those not residing in the clouds, I know and hang-out with much smaller women who possess pounds of confidence and self-esteem. As one Sage Story points out, how we feel on the inside is displayed on our outside. I also provide frank information and truths about cleavage and its proper place at work. People talk about breasts, cleavage, and, sadly, make judgment calls about our values regarding this part of our anatomies. Worry not, though, you will be "uplifted" with my pearls of wisdom and ideas for action!

Like a treasure chest filled with gold and jewels, **Chapter 9** addresses professional clothing, workplace perceptions based on how we choose to dress ourselves, appropriate necklines, of course, and the value of investing in ourselves through a few classic pieces of clothing to stand the test of time and fad. All the while, be assured that I am not telling you what is right or wrong; I am arming you with knowledge and ideas to help my fellow woman. While there may be no single, right answer, be assured that there are countless wrong answers when it comes to our attire because #clothingmatters, #youmatter, and #everyoneknows.

As we scan the entire body, remember that the whole you includes a size and shape consuming space while navigating others' sizes and shapes. Additionally, as you are keenly aware, our whole bodies also emit odors and bodily sounds as part of how we communicate. This seems like the perfect chapter to talk size and smell. Some really nice, and some, not so nice. Again, I'll defer to the research to remind us, wonderful readers in active learning modes that sometimes the message smells. Fret not, though, for there is always another study challenging prior knowledge. Remember, the iconic words of British synthpop band, *The Human League*, that "we're only human and born to make mistakes." People are complicated, so let's help.

Small. Medium. Large. XL. XXL. XXXL.

Yuck.

0. 2. 4. 6. 8. 10. 12. 14. 16. 18. 20. 22. 24.

Better?

Petite. Juniors. Average. Plus.

That's the ticket. Not.

It is no wonder why men and women despise shopping for women's clothing. To set the course for a pending disaster and potential fight of the 21st Century, we even plead with our loved ones to, "Come shopping, it'll be fun."

It is a challenging mess to understand sizes, let alone, find an assigned numeric value to flatter each of our unique body parts. As we begin to grow and appreciate our own physical structures through knowledge, empathy, and acceptance, I include a brief investigation on the body of literature studying this very subject. Like many of you, I am not happy with some of the research or perceptions. Others' mystical powers to control our feelings and nonverbals as bright professionals in the workplace evoke a mass of opinions and feelings from yours truly.

But, really, I predict it isn't much different from what I hear on a daily basis about the battle women fight and promote by emotionally destroying images of the self. Negative speak, poor self-esteem, other female harsh judgments, and the never ending inner feelings of gloom and despair worn on the outside, are daily reminders that our whole person is subject to harm. Sadly, harm far greater than bad air quality, lack of sleep, and a poor diet. This is an assault designed to embed its cancerous tangles in every emotional cell of our fiber. No thanks, I prefer a fiber-rich muffin if that's the case.

With that said, I bring to you a host of research studying women's "body image," coupled with a variety of interesting topics, with the hope that we can glean diamonds from carbon minefields. Again, knowledge is power as we strengthen our nonverbal communication in and out of the workplace with all that we bring.

Body Image + Spirituality

A study asked 124 female college students from Singapore and other Asian countries to rate their spiritual values, life priorities, and images of their bodies through a series of questions and discussions. The results were not surprising in terms of strong spiritual beliefs coupled with centered priorities in life. However, women struggled "in the formation of their body image, a sense of self, relationship building, and connection with the world … reflected by an underlying personal quest to achieve a stable positive self-identity, a larger purpose in life, and a sustained connection with others." Geez. That doesn't sound good. Another group of bright, young, impressionable women half a world away from us battling the same issues that haunt American college women preparing to thrive in life. I suggest we look around. Those college graduates might just be residing in the cubicle, office, or workstation next to you, for all you know. Peek around the corner. Is she there?

Shifting faiths, an Australian team conducted a study on weight, faith, and body images from 189 Muslim and non-Muslim women, ages 18-58. Weight (BMI) and height were self-reported and categorized as either normal, overweight, and obese. A clothing modesty scale and several diet/body/eating disorder questionnaires were administered. The researcher found that, for Muslim women, "strength of religious faith was inversely related to body dissatisfaction, body self-objectification, and dietary restraint." With the assistance of modest clothing and reduced Western media exposure of body images, the relationship between all of these factors was mediated. The author also hinted that limited exposure to Western body images and body ideals was a positive factor for Muslim women. As he put it, "buffering against appearance-based public scrutiny" might have its place for helping women.

Again, we find no surprises that women from differing faiths from around the world are aware of their bodies and how they perceive them. Speaking of perceptions, this next section targets the media which drives multi-million dollar industries eager to swoop in and save us all from ourselves through perceptions and, all too often, deceptions targeting females.

Body Image + The Media

I almost hesitate to wreck our already skewed views of media mongers and advertising firms' abilities to permeate our homes and lives, grab our impressionable loved ones, and lure us into perceptions of cultural norms and ideals. Free shipping, too, if you call in the next 15 minutes. We like to think we can shelter those around us. We also like to think that we are above what they are selling, too. Not so quick, grasshopper!

Rather than provide you with just a study or two, I've included findings from what's called a meta-analysis. In this case, a review of 77 studies yielding a wealth of information. Thank you, dedicated scientists. My hypothesis remains, every so sadly, confirmed that their findings connecting media images depicting the "thin-ideal body" with body image issues remains a big problem for women. So much media saturation has experts affirming that "thin leads women to see this ideal as normative, expected, and central to attractiveness." Many studies verify that we actually feel worse about ourselves after being exposed to thin media models when compared to other images. To beat a dead horse, other bodies of work associated frequent exposure to fashion magazines and television programs with super thin ideal body types. Again, evidence confirms that these subtle assaults are contributing to body dissatisfaction and eating disorders. It's a vicious cycle. Let's dismount.

Not to say this issue is universal for every female walking the planet, because thousands of women possess positive images of themselves; but, sadly, this is not what I typically encounter when I have the pleasure to converse with women. It's rare that I hear women saying things like, "I like the way I look and I feel beautiful and happy just the way I am." There's always just a little tweaking that follows; and, it's frequently hinted around dropping a few pounds. When I hear someone tell me they wish they were taller, I think we have a different issue at hand. Thankfully, media-DNA didn't make me 5'11½".

Moving forward with our whole nonverbal, talkative, and near-perfect bodies, the research carries a strong message. Alarming rates of eating disorders plague us and clear-cut connections between media and body dissatisfaction are obvious. However, an "increased investment in appearance" is something that we can tackle, and prevail, given the right tools and the right support. I say this with great enthusiasm; do not invest financially to change ourselves to meet external standards. Rather, invest in ourselves because we are worth it!

Body Image + Weight

Ok, let's go there – in spite of our possible discomfort. Let's consider the evidenced-based research beyond magazine rack articles and photos to see if we, as women, have different perceptions of ourselves and the blanket of skin and fat cells documented by authentic research.

More than 3,200 adults participated in a study involving telephone call and mailed questionnaires. A broad range of demographic information was obtained for analysis. Participants' average age was 47 and all had normal or higher (18.5+) body mass indexes (BMIs). Forty-eight percent (48%) were women, 88% described themselves as White, and approximately 64% were married. Additional information collected included height, weight, perceived weight, and psychological well-being.

The researchers' findings noted a significant difference between women and men in terms of BMI and well- being. Women with higher BMIs had feelings of less well-being. Men did not feel the same way about themselves. The experts then separated weight into five categories from, normal to obese III, and recalculated. For each of the new distinct weight groups, women still had significantly lower scores of well-being than women with normal weights and, certainly, from their male counterparts. Remember, this is just one study about wellness and weight. Again, the data is significant and not too wonderful for women.

Let's review one more to fully clarify for any human being out there who might think that "women + weight" do not have a life-long relationship to some degree. A peek into something as simple as a magazine study to confirm our suspicions is in order. Ninety women between the ages of 18 and 35 were asked to view magazines featuring three different advertising set-ups: 1. A thin woman; 2. A thin woman with at least one attractive man; and 3. An ad in which no people were featured. The photos had been previously vetted by the researcher in terms of appeal and effectiveness for the study. Participants rated the photos and also completed self-objectification, appearance anxiety and negative mood, and body assessments. It was confirmed that women who viewed thin-themed advertisements had higher levels of anxiety, negative mood, and body dissatisfaction than the control groups.

While no gross injustice was gleaned from the body of work setting off a five-alarm fire, clear evidence continues to suggest a "small, but consistent" effect on women's well-being. Meaning, a little bit goes a long way. Gigantic billboards, video games, social media flooding, fashion show runways, display window mannequins, beauty pageants, and music videos are just a few of the opportunities we are exposed to daily to plant the ideas for how we should see ourselves.

Body Image + Body Odors

As part of your image, indulge me for a moment to talk about chewing gum. Just a sentence or two to help anyone clueless to the fact that our society has gum rules. No chomping. No smacking. No seeing it in your mouth. No bubble blowing during meetings. While we all appreciate fresh breath, take heed that your gum will communicate things about you that you wouldn't want to know. Please be a silent gum chewer. Everyone will appreciate that. And, for Pete's sake (whoever Pete is), do not chew gum when you are presenting in front of an audience. If in doubt, jump ahead to this chapter's Sage Story on the basics of audiences and you, the professional presenter.

Since I opened my mouth about gum, let's also address the issue of body odors and nonverbal implications. No one has to say a word when it comes to smell. We are bloodhounds and can sniff out the best of smells and the worst of smells. How does HR address an employee's body odor issue and the disruption those funky smells are causing? Technically, we know that the odor itself is "created by our apocrine sweat glands." But who cares, something stinks and, "Houston, we have a problem."

The reality is this. Someone has to step-up and talk with this employee about that body odor. Otherwise, negative perceptions of The Stinker will win over brilliant ideas "Glandular Guy" brings to the workplace. My first suggestion is that you take a personal assessment of your own odors. Trustworthy friends and concerned supervisors, who want you to thrive, will be honest about your sweaty reputation if you ask them. The bottom line, "Smells trump Smarts." How's that for a tagline!

Additionally, odors on the other end of the smelly gauge include the over-application of perfumes, lotions, and potions. While these odors will not produce the same effect from others within 25 feet of you, the premise is the same. Between allergies and sensitive smellers, do not overspray or splash. Learn what chemicals react with your skin bacteria to produce a pleasant smell and also, regulate quantity. There's a reason that expensive perfumes are sold by the ounce in tiny little bottles that cost $150; a little bit goes a long way. You should know this as you rip apart every magazine perfume ad and rub the latest fragrance on your arms, or two fragrances, or three. Immediately, discontinue use.

designed by freepik.com

Back to where we started. We cannot overhaul advertising and shift an entire industry to meet our feminist global strategic plan; I admit that. As an industry, they can and do produce phenomenal and inspirational work highlighting solutions for thousands of life's most challenging issues. Many ethical advertising and marketing agencies support community efforts to make our world a better place. I applaud any campaign for helping with a global crisis, or marketing the best car of the year because it makes our lives comfortable and safe. But, I struggle and squawk as the gross decisions made by a room of people who objectify women to make a buck.

Therefore, I challenge you with a little social media trivia, compliments of randomhistory.com, to lighten our brains and provide comic relief. Grab a pen and see how well you do. Answers are provided at the end of the chapter. Call it research.

A. What is the only planet in our solar system with a female name?

B. What is the average height and weight of an American woman?

C. Name the #1 disease killer of women.

D. By the age of 55, what % of women in the US have been married?

E. What state elected the first female governor?

F. What country had the first women to rule a country as an elected leader in the modern era?

G. In this state, it is against the law to remarry the same man four times.

H. Hartford, CT banned men from doing this with their wives on Sunday.

I. The third week of this month is National Singles Week in the US.

J. Studies show that before a man even speaks word, the way he stands (slouching or not) counts for over __% of a woman's first impression.

Ideas to Consider:

1. We come in a variety of sizes and the beauty of that is the fact that people like to have choices. So, while a muscular, fit woman may be the perfect match for her mate, another may prefer tall, dark, and lovely. Embrace and nurture the uniqueness of what embodies you. There's no need to discredit our outside packages, because the **treasures come from within all shapes and sizes**.

2. Recognize that body image does not operate in a vacuum. This complex mental and emotional model we possess is closely tied to how we operate, explore, and receive the world. Take time to understand your personal body image and **imagine the possibilities**.

3. There's no such thing as perfect. You are not and, I guarantee you, I fall far from that word. But, I do things well. I thrive at work, and my brain bursts with life. **Find your perfections in the wrinkles, freckles, and folds of your body language.**

4. The next time you watch a television show or read a magazine article about how to improve you, or what to wear, or 95 ways to drop those extra 5 pounds, save $4, click the off button, or scan for a show highlighting someone driven to cure cancer or help kids. Skip that superficial, Hollywood-driven, unattainable image and look around. The answers aren't in the glossy pages and pixel counts of reality TV shows. **The truths come from within women, and their male support systems who help them, inside and out.**

5. The answers: A. Venus; B. 5'4" and 163 lbs.; C. heart disease; D. approximately 95%; E. Wyoming; F. Sri Lanka; G. Kentucky; H. kissing; I. September; J. 80.

Take-Away:

Body image is still a fight. Take a step in your personal and professional world to shatter the negative images in the mirror and see the carats of diamonds. Even with your flaws, you are priceless.

CARBON INTO DIAMONDS	
Reflections ... *What I gleaned from this chapter*	Personal Action Plan ... *What I plan to do with this new knowledge*

Deanna just called a meeting.
Everyone has an emotional reaction to the thought of her running the agenda.

Sage Story

I have a Pet Peeve! by Janet Dunn

After more than 30 years of being on the receiving end of presentations and keynotes in and out of my organization I have no tolerance for people that make presentations without taking time to know their audience. Allow me to explain this further. From a young age I was involved in formal oratorical training as a member of my high school speech and debate team. In essence I wrote original oratory and presented it in a competitive setting. The people that I presented to were judges, and competitors. It was there that I learned to read my audience. I had to figure out a way to connect with these people who were hearing my presentation with different criteria in mind. I had to be relevant to both groups. After all, a trophy was on the line.

When I worked for the national YMCA I was often asked to deliver keynote and trainings to people within the Y movement. One time, in particular, I was going to be presenting to a group of Y CEO's with tenure in the organization. They were required to take this training as a matter of course, but were far beyond this in their everyday lives. I knew that. I knew that if I delivered this training as the curriculum stated they would be miserable and learning would not take place. So, I improvised. I presented the material from a totally different perspective. And, I did all of that at the last minute. In other words, the decision to train differently was made right as they walked in the door and I listened to their grumbling about having to be there. I listened to my audience.

Recently, at a Rotary meeting, the speaker was a Federal Judge. Although there were other judges and lawyers in the audience, most were not. The presenter talked about the need for the federal courts, but did so in a way that was funny, enlightening and informational. What could have been a disaster was averted because he took the time to know his audience.

Another mistake often made is when the presenter is not aware of the nonverbal clues of the participants. Presenters are so determined to deliver their agenda that they fail to understand that live people are sitting there on the receiving end. It is the nonverbal clues that are most important. Rarely will someone stand up and tell the speaker that they are boring or irrelevant; but, all will tell the speaker through actions just what they think. Things like looking at their watch, falling asleep, yawning, texting or checking email are signs that things aren't going so well. Flexibility and adaptation are two critical elements that good speakers possess. If those nonverbal clues are apparent, a good speaker will do things to wake-up the crowd and will have the ability to change the presentation - in real time - to make it more interesting. They may skip over slides, or ask for audience participation, or even stop and take questions midway through. All of these things will tell your audience that the presenter is "clued in" to their feelings.

It is essential that, when asked to present, be prepared by, 1) Knowing the group that you are speaking to, and 2) Being flexible with Plan B if the material is not being received well. By doing these two things, you can take a presentation to an entirely new level.

CHAPTER 5

ABOVE THE SHOULDERS

Face it. Face the facts. Lights. Camera. Action. Or, basically a day in your life once you step through your front door. The face is a complicated, living billboard expressing our inner thoughts. We know it is challenging to mask our emotions. From grief to anger, our faces communicate without uttering a single word. This chapter provides an in-depth review of studies involving the face, our emotions, and others' perceptions of us. Knowing that our faces are closely tied to how we communicate and interact within our circles, it's worth providing strong evidence about this critical communicator. When I suggest you "put your best face forward," there are good reasons, rooted in science, driving this advice.

A team of European researchers studied the effects of women with and without makeup. Findings did not solely focus on makeup and beauty; fortunately, but also included perceptions of health and confidence. Looking at a series of females with and without facial foundation and eye makeup, participants of both genders found that "female faces were more attractive when they were shown wearing makeup." I know, I know. Do not shoot the messenger (AKA, me). Most likely, makeup enhanced women's uniform skin texture and facial symmetry. We, as humans, are drawn to symmetry and balance in nature; so, body symmetry specific to the face would make sense.

This chapter is not about wearing makeup; or, natural beauties or stunning magazine spreads riddled with dozens of cosmetic advertisements. Rather, my intent is to focus on empowering ourselves by intentionally deciding how we want to present and engage in social settings with our best face forward. The thought of makeup positively impacting a women's well-being and confidence are powerful outcomes and worthy of investigation. Researchers also studied possible connections between cosmetics, health, confidence, earning potentials, and professional classes. Strong results were published in the *Journal of Applied Social Psychology*. For the sake of helping each other reach our earning potentials and real or perceived professional class (status), I share the highlights. The following captures the variables used to gauge participants' perceptions when measured against a series of photographs:

Status:	Typically Associated Jobs
High	Accountant, Architect, Company Director
Average	Bank Clerk, Customer Service, Graphic Designer
Lower	Childcare, Cleaner, Factory Worker
Other	Unemployed

Participants were asked to compare computer images of women and rate makeup/no makeup with professions. The findings were fascinating! They found that "wearing makeup had a significant impact on the rating of a woman's professional class." Those wearing makeup were labeled of higher status. Photographs of women without makeup, however, were categorized with lower status jobs. I am not saying this is fair or right or just. I am saying that knowledge and choices are important as to how we deliberately engage with our body language and our work-related ambitions. No doubt that for every study encouraging or promoting facial attention, another study will, and should, challenge the findings. I did, though, appreciate the earning potential category as a part of this study. Most of us in the workplace want to increase our earnings and gain the advantage.

Again, financial specific outcomes found that, "When wearing cosmetics, women were also assigned greater earning potential and considered to have more prestigious jobs than when they were presented without makeup." I can hear some of you grumbling at what may seem the ridiculousness of judgment and makeup. Therefore, I suggest we focus on ensuring that our image is exactly what we want to bring to every social and professional situation. For me, there will be no makeup while walking the block in my tennis shoes; but, a little eyeliner and blush covers a multiple of California sun damage tanning adventures and well-earned wrinkles for this youthful 50 year old during speaking engagements!

To add to this important component of how we communicate, numerous first impression studies suggest or conclude that our faces communicate information in less than one second and significantly impact our perceptions of other people. One Princeton University team studied the simple conditions of facial exposure, lengths of time, and judgments of attractiveness, likeability, trustworthiness, competence, and aggressiveness. Want to guess the results from these multiple studies? I'll highlight.

1. We make judgments about people in a mere 1/10th of a second (first glance).

2. With a little extra time, just a second or two more, our judgments tend to become more negative about the person we just encountered.

3. Our confidence levels specific to these judgments increase with a little extra time. Think about the impact of these three points and your first impression.

Findings from the University of Pennsylvania add to the rich body of nonverbal data and social psychology. Their research linked appearance as an important element for encounters and garnishing information about gender, age, culture, class, job, group membership, personality, interpersonal attitudes, feelings, and social roles. Wow! Basically, they concluded that "what we look like can affect what others think of us, how we see ourselves, and how we attract others to us."

Their work targeted specific issues impacting most of us on a daily basis. Cosmetics, hair care, same/different perceptions by men and women, and positive self-esteem categories were included in their work. With a wealth of information, statistically significant data, and consistent findings, I must admit that I wasn't sure as to where to start in helping shape this book and empower you, as engaging women with strong opinions and even stronger feelings. It is my intention to provide knowledge specific to these characteristics without pouring over pages from great minds and spewing jargon to impress. Therefore, allow me to point out a few results from their multi-study findings as <u>areas to consider</u>:

- ✓ The use of cosmetics is important in influencing daily encounters and promoting our psychological well-being - particularly as we age.

- ✓ Facial makeup is associated with impressions of being "outgoing" and care of our hair is linked to perceptions of our gentler (softer) personality.

- ✓ Perfume and mascara play important social roles based on genders and situations.

- ✓ Wearing makeup at night is considered "more attractive" given specific settings.

- ✓ The role of makeup in recovering from illness positively impacts feelings of self-worth.

- ✓ Cosmetic procedures can have an overall favorable psychological effect and benefit a person's life.

Consider that we make first impressions every day. From job interviews to casual run-ins at the grocery store, we are continuously sizing-up people and they are doing the same. We know the power of this because social media has a field day plastering inappropriate photos of people in different social settings and inviting comments. You know what I mean. We are bombarded with these visual images on a daily basis and they appear on every device in our environment. So, I ask you, what is the image you want to put out there for others? What, as smart, engaging, and worthy women do you want to project on your billboard? Again, this is not about judgment in the sense of being a "judge-y person." Rather, it's the basic requirement of our physical safety and security imperative to our physical bodies when we encounter other people. We, as homo sapiens, must judge our environment for basic safety.

Work conducted at my alma mater, the University of California - Riverside, provided dynamic information linked to our nonverbal world and how we are perceived. Purposely not including validity and reliability details to bore even the most veracious reader, correlations between self-esteem, health, smiling, stance, and open arms improved others' views of us, as well as perceptions of ourselves. Frustratingly though, their findings pointed-out that gender plays a negative role for women regarding indicators of conscientiousness. Men were, under certain static conditions, rated higher in terms of neater appearance, looking healthier, and having a more distinctive appearance.

I challenge that though. I think you are eagerly nodding your head, too. We know that education is powerful and with a helpful spirit and the right intentions, women can and should equal their male counterparts in terms of appearance, health, and distinction. Doing so, however, is easier said than done. It can be exhausting under the microscope. All of us despise the perceptions of some ill-intentioned individuals telling us all about our bodies, personalities, and emotional well-being. As we point the finger at someone else, remember, three more fingers are pointing back at you. Alright, enough soapbox.

Hair. Hair. Everywhere.

That's me. I have that cotton-candy, fly away 80s hair that soaks-up a can of AquaNet like water to a malnourished cactus. Without a blast of lacquer post-styling, I make no promises as to my hair at the end of a busy day. What about you? Whether we pulled the short, thin straw in the hair department or the thick, course beautiful mane similar to a mountain lion, hair care matters. People notice. Office workers talk about ponytails, oily strands, bad haircuts, color choices, facial hair, eyebrow hair, nose hair, chin hair … ok, I'll stop. I think it's fair to say that hair deserves our attention because it communicates a bundle of information.

As you primp and fuss, or maybe not, during your morning routine, consider your hair as the frame for your face to ensure that you are a one-of-a-kind photograph. I can guarantee that, if you decide to opt out of hairstyle day, your colleagues (and strangers, for the record) will be more than happy to giggle, comment, judge, secretly photograph, or something of the sort, about your hairdo. Duke University research even found that this whole hair bias thing aligned with judgments of competence, intelligence, trustworthiness, and, yes, deciding how amiable we are perceived. Throw in hiring, promotions, and performance appraisals and the tangle's amass. Research also confirms that women actually "suffer a disadvantage in crafting this professional image due to negative stereotypes, lower expectations, and workplace norms." To think, I thought a neatly plastered ponytail would do the trick. Apparently not.

I read about an African-American woman who wore her hair in braids and dreadlocks to the office. She was fired. Yes, fired. I'd like to write that these types of egregious lawsuits are rare, but such is not the case. Do a Google search and you'll see many lawsuits about hair, perceived professional image, and minority women receiving the brunt force of this discrimination. One person's interpretation of "eye catching" hairstyles apparently did not appreciate the "finger waves" as acceptable for the professional workplace. It makes me think about my own hair with zero finger waves. Or, just how blonde I want to go this month? Should I conform? Buck the system? Both have positive and negative consequences. I'm staying blonde thanks to hair foiling and that's that. For the record, hair color, as well as hair length, research topics are also popular and yield useful information.

Another body of research targeted women's hairstyles and men's behavior. I feel you starting to grin and what that might possibly mean. In all, 90 men and 90 women between the ages of 25 and 45 were studied as they walked alone down a pedestrian trail. The actress (known as the confederate, in research speak) would then walk towards a participant coming towards her and, subtly seek eye contact with the stranger. She would then "accidentally drop her glove without realizing it." Researchers tracked who would retrieve the glove based on the confederate's particular hairstyle.

This scenario was repeated. The only detail changed was specific to the way her was hair styled into one of three conditions: natural, ponytail, or bun. Want to guess the results? Men, but not really women, offered to retrieve the glove more often when the confederate's hair fell naturally on her shoulders compared to a ponytail or bun style. So, all of those silky, shiny, free flowing, manes of hair bouncing around shampoo commercials might be based in a little science conditioned with perception and gender.

Speaking of hair, let's go past the obvious hair on our heads as part of our image. Facial and body hair are also topics for workplace conversations. From tufts exploding from a colleague's nostrils to the iconic uni-brow, how do we gingerly address this subject without subjecting ourselves to acting like the health class hygiene heroine? I might also add the same attention be given for chin and ear hair. Chin strands tend to be a popular location for Gen X and Baby Boomer women enjoying bursts of testosterone and boar-like hairs with a brief return to adolescence. Seriously, the business of hair changes people's perceptions for how we groom ourselves.

Look Into My Eyes

The eye business is rather eye-opening. A friend of mine recently paid $908 for a pair of prescription glasses. Really? A mortgage payment. None the less, taking care of our eyes is serious business and the professionals know this. As Mom said, "You only have one pair, so don't go poking them out." As for eyes as nonverbal communicators, our eyes, proverbially speaking, are the windows into our souls. I've seen tears of joy, loss, and a slew of other emotions through the power of our eyes. Learning how to read others' eyes and the frame around them will benefit you throughout your life.

Did you know that you cannot make your pupils grow intentionally? Of course, exposing them to light and dark will make them shrink and expand, but beyond that, look in the mirror and 'will' your pupils to grow. Pupils are, however, triggered by our emotions. When we like something, our pupils expand. When we don't, they retract or shrink. Think about this during a meeting. Your colleague is excited about the new project. You even notice that her eyes "light up" as she's grinning excessively and clapping her hands. In reality, her happy-pupils are doing the happy-dance. Her genuine emotions are being immediately expressed through her eye language and pupil size. Be on the lookout and you'll begin to notice how others' pupils align with their feelings. Also, take note that your own pupils will call-you-out if your inner feelings and your outward behaviors don't match. Don't be a bad pupil.

Another attribute about our eyes pertains to our sclera – the whites of our eyes. We don't really pay attention to this part of our eyes until the white part doesn't look really white. You've seen this before. Blood shots eyes and you're thinking, "Someone's been up too late, or having a good time." Watery eyes and their owner scratching too often makes you question, "Allergies?" And, when the white part isn't snow white, our subconscious takes note and wonders if that person is sick. These are all natural reactions for responding to the physical condition of our eyes.

Touching upon the sensitivity of our peepers, remember, "Don't shoot until you see the whites of their eyes." Wait. Don't judge until you've asked about the whites of their eyes. Just because a person has bloodshot eyes does not mean they are 'under the influence.' Maybe those "peepers" are exhausted from reading all weekend, or getting up with Baby at 2:00, 3:00, 4:00, and 5:00 AM. Take a moment to check on someone with questionable eyes; they talk to us anyway. As a reminder, check thyself. If your eyes are crying out, literally or figuratively, before your next meeting, decide how you want to address this. Eye drops? Disclosure of your emotions driving those tears? Or, a reschedule until those beautiful Big Brown, Gorgeous Green, or Baby Blues feel and look better?

Just as you are wise to not judge a book by its cover, think about our eyes and the cover, or frame, around such cover. Eyebrows, bags, and lines add details to the nonverbal messages of our eyes. While I personally value those well-earned lines, the condition of our eyebrows is, as mentioned earlier, part of our hair care. Research confirms that the role of our eyebrows goes well beyond offering modest protection from sweat and rain; these two important arches of hair "appear to play an important role in the expression of emotions and the production of other social signals."

Good information to know as you grab your tweezers, examine your own brows, and decide how these little caterpillars should arch above your eyes. Experimental results from the research suggest that this region of our face may be as influential as the eyes themselves. As you ponder this, picture someone without eyebrows. Or, recall a colleague sporting a Cro-Magnon uni-brow. In either case, reflect on how we perceive and receive this person. Even Brooke Shields's eyebrows became a trendy topic in the 80s. Regardless, know that the well-groomed eyebrow may be worthy of waxing as part of our nonverbal facial language and the image we wish to bring to the forefront.

Eyeglasses also help us understand someone and how we read their intensions. First made in Italy (don't we just love the Italians), eyeglasses had and continue to have an important role in global society. From function to fashion, we proudly place these artifacts upon our face to express a myriad of feelings and thoughts. Functionally, you may need them to read, or fashionably, you may like a particular designer. In either case, wearing glasses tells us something about the wearer.

Studies on wearing glasses and the reasons for it are fairly simple. We like the way they make us look and, more often than not, we think they make us looker smarter. But, why would we think this? The formula is simple:

> **Smart people** read a lot.
> When you read a lot, your eyes go bad.
> When your eyes go bad, you **need glasses**.
> Therefore, smart people need glasses.

I know, not exactly rocket science, but fairly accurate rationale according to the experts. Several studies confirm the stereotypes, first impressions, and intellectual expectations we place on people who wear glasses. Without giving you a prescription to invest in a pair of glasses, think about glasses in your life. Sunglasses. Readers. Bi-focals. None, because you opted for contacts. Whatever the case, know that this facial artifact, encasing your eyes, is part of how you communicate and often the subject of off-the-record chitchat about how they look on you.

Smile, Lips, and Teeth

"Smile, you're on *Candid Camera*." Not really. OK, really. Cameras are all around us and, even before those memory makers were capturing our every move, our smiles captured the attention of other people. We know that smiling is a universal symbol representing trust, warmth, and welcoming feelings. So, how often do you smile? Are you hesitant to flash your smile because someone might judge you? There's much to be learned from mastering our smiles based on the research. Know that we use different smiles depending on the situation, as well as the type of smile we flash. We have the ability to produce a genuine (Duchenne) smile or disingenuous grin. I've summarized a few of the benefits that we, as professionals, gain if we work hard to flash a genuine smile.

People who genuinely smile are perceived as more:

1. Trustworthy
2. Persuasive
3. Likeable
4. Attractive

Those simple perceptions, alone, would make me want to produce a warm and authentic smile. Not sure how to smile a Duchenne smile? The formula is simple: Simultaneously, contract your zygomatic major muscles with your orbicularis oculi muscles. Huh? In simple terms, use your mouth muscles and your eye muscles to express a genuine smile. Simply pulling the sides of your mouth into a smile-arch of some sort does not constitute an authentic smile. We read this particular part of someone's body language quickly by looking at both the mouth muscles and the little crinkles at the ends of our eyes to indicate if the smile is bona fide. A plastic surgeon, and in particular, this chapter's Sage Story, is an artist when it comes to smiles and muscles. While he can skillfully help with our bodies, be wise to know that our insides and outsides are still there once the bandages come off.

We all know a fake smile when we see it. We usually fake smile back while our brains are mentally exiting the exchange or thinking unpleasant thoughts. Promise yourself that you will not be that person. Crinkle those eyes, like good jolly ol' Kris Kringle, and let your receiver know that you mean business. Your smile legitimizes your positive nonverbal image. As a part of this, remember to also take care of the frame around your smile – your lips.

Don't give me any lip service. A moment or two talking about lip care is important. Women are masters for using their lips via lipstick application, lip color, chewing, and touching. In terms of nonverbal communication, our lips help with our verbal language and either: 1. Support our message, or 2. Sabotage us.

Observe people and just watch their mouths and lips. Do they chew on their lips? This may be a sign on nervousness. Do they constantly lick them? It could be that they are just dry or, perhaps are they "licking their chops" in anticipation of something. Watch for symmetry between the left side and right side of the mouth. We usually talk symmetrically, so when I notice a slight elevation on one side, something is going on in their brain. A shift from the norm; a break from the baseline – those ever so subtle micro-expressions come to life. When you see this, look for other nonverbal cues leaking from their bodies to help us understand what they are <u>really</u> saying. If these match with the spoken words, then I suggest we move on. If they don't match, it's time for Inspector Gadget.

I will not make light of teeth and how they impact our image; the physical health of our teeth is important and we are judged by their condition. I'm the first to say that dental care is expensive and thousands are unable to care for their teeth. In the workplace, a beautiful, straight, mouth of white choppers is ideal, but rare. Whatever you were born with, straightened, or bleached over time, dental care is important for our body image. While you may not be able to afford braces or have a row of porcelain crowns for that Hollywood smile, you can, and should ensure that your dental habits are top notch.

Know that un-flossed teeth produce odors over time and plaque is an unpleasant topic, to say the least. But, people will talk about your teeth. If a front tooth is missing from a weekend of partying, as depicted in *The Hangover*, I can promise you that it will be THE topic of conversation on every work email, bathroom conversation, and nonverbal water cooler huddle.

Ideas to Consider:

1. Life isn't a beauty contest; however, it is a "best in show" opportunity. So, show up and be your best.

2. Appreciate the value of first impressions for our physical safety, but own the fact that these same impressions are made by others about us. What impressions do you want to initially make and how will you enhance these through your verbal and nonverbal cues?

3. Be a sight for sore eyes.

4. Take care of your physical body, inside and outside. We are living organisms and external forces constantly bombard us. Have a health assessment and follow Dr.'s orders. Ok, I'm not *that* kind of doctor, but I do have great advice to help us thrive.

Take-Away:

Face it. The face matters and so does its crowning glory. Make educated decisions about both. As you promote women, know that your feminism philosophy fights for all that is equal to that of men; and we can advocate while wearing a bit of mascara.

CARBON INTO DIAMONDS	
Reflections ... *What I gleaned from* *this chapter*	Personal Action Plan ... *What I plan to do with* *this new knowledge*

IDIOM EPISODE #5

Charged with developing a new concept for the firm, the team quickly realizes that they're not on the same page as yesterday. Frustration is obvious, but cooler heads prevail as the six plow through their action items.

Sage Story

Matching the Inside with the Outside by Carey Nease

As a cosmetic and facial plastic surgeon I have the opportunity to affect the lives of both men and women in a positive manner; particularly in regards to their appearance. I have been in practice for 13 years and have consulted with and operated on more than 8,000 people, of which about 90% are women between the ages of 25-65. Most of my patients come in for an evaluation and procedure that will help them feel more confident with one or more aspects of their appearance. The reasons for each visit vary. From wanting to look younger, or hoping to improve the relationship with their spouse or significant other, their reasons are as unique as them. Some just want to be more effective in the workplace; which I noticed is most common among the men in my practice. In general, though, people just want to look as good as they feel. The saying, "50 is the new 30" rings true in my experience. And, there is no doubt that women, now more than ever, are driven to be attractive and youthful. Social media is driving this trend and there is no end in sight.

There are a multitude of reasons I enjoy my profession, but the most rewarding is empowering women to be self-confident in all aspects of their lives. There are 2 typical groups who ask for help. The first is the young or middle-aged mom who has lost that feeling of confidence in the appearance of her body compared to pre-pregnancy or younger days. Having children is a blessing, but the physical toll it takes on the mother's body can be significantly unappealing and distressing from her perspective. This often affects the relationship with her spouse/significant other. Sadly, struggles in these relationships are common; sometimes even resulting in divorce. What follows is also commonly destructive behavior: worsening health problems, obesity, promiscuity, and depression. The opportunity I have to restore their body to their pre-pregnancy state is rewarding to me and brings unbelievable value for these women. I have seen revitalization of marriages, higher self-confidence and self-esteem, improved energy, the drive to be healthy and active, and even reversal of depression after performing procedures related to the affects of childbirth.

Similarly, women and men who have lost a significant amount of weight struggle with their appearance and self-confidence. This group is like the young mother with changes in body aesthetics, but different in that, for many cases, they have already done amazing things to improve their health and lifestyle. My role is to finish the job they started. These patients are commonly motivated, confident, and have a positive outlook on their future in nearly all aspects. Their relationships thrive, they are successful in the workforce, and often, become motivators to others who are in the position they once were but have overcome. It is a privilege to assist these patients in improving their lives.

Another group seeking my expertise includes older women and men looking aged, but feeling young, active, and want to maintain their appearance. The most common statement I hear is, "I look in the mirror and wonder who that old woman is staring back at me." For men, they simply want to look youthful in order to compete in the workforce. Many men in their 60s are still healthy, active, and interested in working; particularly in sales positions. Enhancing their appearance or simply maintaining a confident and refreshed look is important for these men. They often get promotions and raises if they appear to be able to continue to be productive in their jobs.

Women, wanting to match the inside with the outside, rarely ask for an over-done look or to resemble a celebrity. Instead they show me photos of themselves 15-20 years prior and hope to regain some of their former vitality and beauty. A youthful face is beautiful, and restoring that sense of beauty is extremely *powerful for making a woman feel captivating. This feeling cannot be underestimated; and I am fortunate to be able to achieve this in many cases. The most common aspects of a woman's face I restore are the brows, eyes, lips, cheeks and neck. The eyes are said to be the window to the soul, and there is no doubt that this feature is the first to be noticed. Youthful eyes are wide-set, slightly slanted (up), open and bright. Whereas, aged eyes are sunken, dull and narrow or down-turned on the outer aspect. Eyebrows should be moderately high and softly arched with fullness. Apple cheeks (full, round, and rosy) are a sign of youth and beauty; soft transitions to the lips and neck are appealing as well. The lips should be full and balanced. The neck should be supple, but without significant skin excess in the midline or along the jaw line. Overall, a youthful face should be oval or heart shaped and full with soft lines and transition zones from one area to the other.*

In describing the above, the opportunity to empower women (and men) with my skill set as a cosmetic surgeon is evident. I am rewarded daily with hugs and thank you cards. I am reminded routinely that what I do can have a tremendous impact on how a person perceives themselves; specifically, in regards to their appearance. All of this translates to their personal relationships, business successes, daily attitudes, and overall self-confidence. If I can help those I encounter in my profession feel more confident, then I will feel like I have used my talents well.

CHAPTER 6

HANDS, ARMS, AND SPACE CONSUMPTION

All hands on deck. Put 'er there! Keep your hands off me. Raise your hands in the air like you just don't care. The list is endless when it comes to how our hands, arms, and upper bodies talk with other people. We all have that special someone who talks with their hands while their mouth is moving. Maybe you're even 'that' special someone! Regardless, movements expressed by our upper bodies have distinct meanings. Researchers at Oregon State University found close ties between hands, handshakes, and personalities which influence outcomes specific to first impressions and judgments.

The biggest complaint and comments I receive from men pertain to one area of women's bodies ... our handshakes. And, hating to be the bearer of bad news ... many women have lousy handshakes. Just think about the days when the power of one's handshake secured the tractor loan or the handshake exchange determined one's character. Well, we haven't changed much since the good ol' days. We are still judged by our handshakes. The Oregon State study actually found that "conscientiousness was judged more accurately when participants shook hands with the targets than when they did not." What this basically means, in a nutshell, is that handshakes carry power and judgment. We should shake hands ... and do it well.

Let me ask, "Were you present in elementary school on handshake day?" No is most likely your answer because there wasn't a handshake day at 99.9% of elementary schools. Nowhere in our formal years and countless hours in school did we study the basics of handshakes. However, in our culture, handshakes are expected and we attach value to this important action. So, fear not, handshake help for mastery is on the way and, before you know it, your handshake will mirror the image you want to project.

Rooted in hundreds of hand and handshake data, findings confirm that handshakes should be a part of our professional introduction and departure from most meetings – particularly with mixed gender encounters. It is not acceptable for our male counterparts to receive hearty handshake welcomes and we, ready for that same welcome, receive a mere nod of the head. Or, even worse, a slight wave of hello, like a pageant contestant. No. No. It's our responsibility to thrust our arm forward and set the bar for how we want to make a first impression. Even dating back to 1940, etiquette expert Emily Post preached about the power of a handshake. Specifically, "the proper handshake is made briefly; but there should be a feeling of strength and warmth to the clasp, and as in bowing, one should at the same time look into the countenance of the persona whose hand one takes." Skip the bowing part.

Countless companies of men cringe at the thought of shaking a woman's hand and will stay clear at all costs until her hand extends first. You can almost hear a sigh of relief from our male counterparts that this first physical encounter will go well because you, the woman in the room, took the initiative to engage. Not sure of this? Take an informal assessment from the males in your world and ask them about shaking women's hands. I think you'll be quite surprised and begin to make some connections between generational differences, expectations, social and professional environments, and expectations.

Now that you possess a clear pounding and understanding about the value surrounding the all important handshake, let us shift our attention as to what strong and communicative handshakes look and feel like from both the giver and receiver's points of view. The techniques for shaking hands involve the whole body, from face to feet, but let me start with the basics of which most of us know.

Our hands. First of all, hands come in a variety of sizes, from mitts to delicate and meaty to slender. What's your anatomical structure? For me, I'm a mitt and own this. I know going in for that first impressionable handshake that there is a high likelihood that shaking a man's hand will feel "equal" from both perspectives. I am eager to shake because I am keenly aware that my hands are bigger than the average female's hands. Take a moment and look at your hands. Seriously, set down this book and examine your hands. Willowy with boney knuckles? Thick and powerful? Long tapers? Soft and fleshy? Ok, pick the book back up and continue.

As you look at your hands, take a brief moment to determine what another person's hands may look and feel like. Big, brawny hands extending from power arms? Or slight, willowy fingers extending from lean arms? Something in between, perhaps? Regardless, knowing what type of physical hand you'll encounter can prove important in terms of pressure, pump time, impression, and overall delivery. Begin to think about what a great handshake looks and feels like. Recall the three little bears. Was the pressure too firm, too mushy, or just right from your shaking partner? This is something most men despise; a woman' soft, raggedy doll-like, delicate hand barely making an introduction. In fact, making <u>quite</u> the impression and not too good, I might add. Remember, a handshake is an extension of you. This is the first time you decide to put forth the effort to make physical contact with someone. No different than eye contact and a genuine smile, let your handshake be memorable for all the right reasons.

Mastering your handshake requires a little time and a lot of practice. I present for your consideration a checklist for your brain and body as you hone your professionalism with a handshake to back it up.

- ☐ Walk towards the person while making eye contact and with a warm smile to set the scene. Let the other person know that a handshake is well on its way.

- ☐ Slow down and stop within an arm's distance of the person while making sure that no barrier, like a chair or desk, blocks this opportunity. If you are sitting when someone enters the room, stand up. Formal handshakes require two standing participants.

- ☐ Extend your right hand at least half way into the shared space. Almost instinctively, the other person will do the same. You might have to hold this position for a second or two in case they weren't sure a woman was going to initiate a handshake.

- ☐ Now this is the important part. With a vertical palm, slide your hand along the person's fingers and through the palm until your thumbs hook. Officially, this is known as the purlicue. Once, you feel this, take your fingers, all of them, and curl around the other person's palm. A mutual grip will ensue. Purlicue to purlicue, both hands are equally engaged.

- ☐ Within a second or two, decide how firmly you want to grip the hand. Think of PSI (pounds per square inch). There's usually a relationship between a person's PSI and their size. Smaller people have lighter squeezes; bigger people have harder grips. Both men and women are keenly aware of this, and will usually comment (after the fact) if the pressure was too much, or too little. If you are a smaller person, you may want to intentionally increase pressure to complement your recipient's hand. On the other hand, if your beastly hand could squash a polar bear's paw, lighten up. Women hate ring imprints on their side fingers. Men detest the thought of pulverizing a delicate wallflower hand.

☐ As you move to pumping the hands, like water from a well, take notice of the degree of aggressiveness specific to this custom. Several (between 5-7) pumps are acceptable in our culture. Too many and you're perceived as eager and destructive. Too few and you're not really enjoying the handshake. Also, watch the shaking factor as it pertains to the rest of the other person's body. Ensure that your recipient's rotator cuff is preserved via non-aggressive pumping.

☐ Elbow etiquette requires that the bend in the elbow extend well beyond 90 degrees, but does not stiff-arm the other person with a thrusting 180 action indicating that they should stay back.

☐ A brief discussion regarding other body parts specific to your handshake: torso, hips, and legs. In what direction are they facing? An authentic person brings 100% full frontal to demonstrate openness. A side shoulder approach might indicate to the other person that it's not worth your time to shift and fully participate. As for the pelvis, again, both hips present with no hints of tilting, leaning, or thrusting which may send the wrong message.

☐ Finally, your feet. A fully present person nonverbally shows this from top to bottom. You've mastered the smile, made great eye contact, your handshake is equal, fitting, and absent of sweat. It's going great and to confirm this, your feet will go where your mind wants to go. Make a mental point to confirm that your feet point towards the person. Feet talk, and you want your feet to convey that you are all-in with this handshake contract.

☐ Practice. Practice. Practice with a trusted man and woman. Solicit feedback and make adjustments.

designed by freepik.com

As we continue to understand the power communicated with our hands, a report on gestures offers glimpses into the world beyond the thumbs' up or middle finger to indicate our motives. As Desmond Morris points out with his human gestures writings, deciding what to include in this book may be pointless since many gestures are so well known. A basic formula helps us understand how we interpret hand gestures: Meaning (message) + Action (movement) + Origin (history) + Locality (culture). Universal gestures may seem like no-brainers for us, au contraire; each has a unique meaning based on the sender and receiver.

Some gestures which support some of our western/American feelings:

Easy

What it sounds like:	What it looks like:
"Back away." Or, anger.	Hands on the hips and the elbows protrude
"I'm gonna' bust your mouth."	Shaking your first towards someone's face
"I promise."	Pointer and middle finger crossed
"Well, hello, good looking."	Lackadaisically stroking and rearranging one's hair

Not so easy

What it sounds like:	What it looks like:
"I'm so frustrated!"	Raising a single strand of hair above your head
"Wait a minute. Time out."	A vertical hand (I) touches the horizontal hand (-)=(T)
"I don't feel good."	Back of your hand presses on your forehead. Close your eyes and slightly tilt back your head
"Let me think about it."	Fingertips together brought to the lips. Rest mouth on top of fingers like a praying position

Difficult (usually origin specific)

What it sounds like:	What it looks like:
"Shut your mouth."	Hand raised and fingers clamp down against the thumb
"I swear." (promise)	First two fingers on each hand crossed over one another
"I smell something fishy."	Raise the hand beside your head and rotate back & forth
"Let's get a drink, friend."	Flick your finger against a friend's neck in the back

While these images may be fairly easy to describe for our mental models, more often than not we accidentally offend someone with our own gestures. From finger pointing to a raised palm placed close to your face, negative gesturing can extract bad feelings from the receiver. While you may not be offended with a scolding finger for ruining the copier, a colleague may feel like a naughty child when, in actuality, the finger pointer indicated frustration. In the words of a memorable teacher, "Sticks and stones may break your bones, but words will never hurt you." Really? I believe that aggressive behaviors (sticks) and fast flying, raging hands and in-your-face (stones) can, in fact, hurt.

What is your style regarding gesturing? Do you look like the office mime, or do you cautiously use your fingers, hands, and body gestures to accentuate and validate your message? Watch savvy politicians and their use of hand gestures. How they "make their point" with poised fingertips, and speak of an emotional event with their hands near their hearts, do not go unnoticed by our subconscious. Notice how they shift from an aggressive finger point towards the camera to a softer finger tip touch without missing a beat? We, in general, enjoy a good story when it's enhanced with purposeful gestures.

If you question your own use of gestures and how they support or challenge your verbal and nonverbals, I suggest one or two activities. Enlist the help of trusted friends and ask them to watch you. Deliver a speech and ask them to only watch your gesturing as you work through your presentation. A critique from gentle sources on the preparation side of a presentation may save you moments of embarrassment later. If you opt to not have your non-judgmental friends judge you, then set-up a camera and video yourself. Go through your entire presentation with the camera recording your every moment. Then, honestly assess yourself. Not only will you be intensely aware of your gestures, but you will notice subtle shifting or rocking, placement of your arms and legs, tone and inflection, and all of the nonverbal activities supporting, or devaluing your verbal message. Perhaps friends will be kinder.

Look closer to hand movements, gesturing, and arms, and reflect how our arms operate while delivering a message. Consider how wide our arms are when stretched horizontally. I'm 6 feet tall; therefore, my arm span is approximately 6 feet wide. That's a lot of geography in a room when my arms are flying around in excitement. Do I really need to thrust them here and there to drive home my message? Was the fish really thatttttt big?

As wonderfully emotional and animated women with great storytelling minds, our ability to enhance our message with exploding arm movements and interpretive dance poses may not go so well at the workplace. Some environments associate employees who incessantly "talk with their hands and arms" as emotional or out of control. While interesting to watch, like a display of flamingos dancing in shallow waters, this may not be the case in many professional, air-conditioned offices with Barry Manilow crooning clients and team members throughout the work day.

However, the skilled professional you present to the workplace knows, or will learn, how to masterfully capture your listeners' attention through subtly choreographed arm gestures, movements, and space consumption. With a few intentional arm movements, your nonverbal image will be enhanced. Thought provoking research on this subject specific to being authentic, particularly at the workplace, highlighted connections for displaying fake or authentic feelings. Fifty consultants were interviewed about their thoughts regarding frantic versus passive behaviors exhibited at their respective firms. Guess what? While the authentic self, outside the corporate culture, was filled with frantic and authentic activity, the contemporary workplace separates the authentic self from the corporate self. Meaning, we should behave a certain way depending on where we are.

Be the flamingo all you want when dancing with fellow flamingos; but at work, watch the flock. Take caution as to how wide you spread your wings, literally. Few appreciate showing of one's tail feathers.

Ideas to Consider:

1. Long before we talk with spoken words, we learned to communicate through squirming, screaming, and stomping to express ourselves. Remember these baby behaviors and remember not to use them at work. No one wants to pacify a tantrum. On the other hand, it makes for a great show.

2. Raise your hand and be noticed by perfecting your handshake. As a part of you, ensure that your handshake is ready for any situation. It will leave a lasting impression.

3. Part of our hands includes nail and skin care. While not the focus of a handshake, when the recipient steps back to evaluate your handshake and you, cleanliness and care are subtle indicators

of how we use these evolutionary tools. No one appreciates a sandpaper handshake because you thought moisturizing wasn't important. The dry times are over and many restrooms provide a pump of relief.

4. Gesturing reinforces our message, good and bad. Take notice of who's watching your conversation from 15' away simply based on your choice of hand and body movements.

<u>Take-away:</u>

Your handshake is an extension of you – make it a good one. Check your gestures to ensure that they convey their intended meanings.

CARBON INTO DIAMONDS	
Reflections ... *What I gleaned from* *this chapter*	Personal Action Plan ... *What I plan to do with* *this new knowledge*

After a grueling four hour work session with management, Dana and Jerome emerge from the meeting with the plans in place, and both feeling that their contributions mattered.

Sage Story

My Hand, My Brand by Gladys Pineda-Loher

When I decided to migrate from my hometown of Manizales, a medium size city in the middle of the Andes of Colombia, South America to Knoxville, TN back in 1998, little did I realize how my life was going to dramatically change. A new culture. A new language. A new way to communicate. A foreigner in a new country, I had to research and learn about this new culture, its customs, and its costumes. The process of assimilation started the moment I landed on American soil; my journey began by using a language different than my native tongue. Keep in mind, I started learning English at an early age; in fact, I had English every school year in South America.

I was taught primarily by Hispanic teachers who were trained using the British English system. I was confident that I could communicate well, in any environment. In my mind, I thought being a successful student in my English classes, plus my job skills for welcoming delegations, diplomats, and visitors who came in Colombia for business, were enough reasons to warrant success in Tennessee. I just knew communication wasn't going to be a challenge for me.

Quickly, I learned that I was wrong. I found myself frustrated by the fact that my accent (and others' accents) was the first roadblock that I had to face in order to understand and be understood.

I was living in an apartment close to campus and it was the perfect location to practice and learn about this new culture. Little did I know how much my nonverbal communication was going to come in hand during this period of acculturation!

From the beginning of my academic, social, and professional life here in the USA until now, I found that in my efforts to understand and being understood, I relied on my hands, eyes, arms, and facial expressions in every situation. One of my coworkers made me aware that I was speaking with my hands; it was not a criticism, for me, it was an eye opener. In that moment, I started to self assess the changes I was making assimilating to a new culture. At an early age, I used to recite poems; I enjoyed moving my arms and trying to convey my message with facial expressions to bring the poem to life. It was a fun, theatrical exercise. I also remember how I used those expressions for memorizing the poems. It seemed that here, now fully living in the USA, it was happening all over again. Except this time, it wasn't just for one poem - it was part of my day to day expressions, and a part of the new me.

Soon, I realized that my cultural behaviors could impact my relationships and my professional life. Learning others' behaviors and their cultures was interesting because I became more aware of similarities and differences. My new journey started by just standing and watching. Later, I become a cultural trainer; in fact, I obtained a certification that gave me the opportunity to study more cultures. As a result, I could see the positive and negative impact of these important nonverbal messages beyond the English language. I saw, too, the impact our non-tangible elements were for making or breaking the deal.

A crucial moment in my career happened at the Hispanic Chamber of Commerce of East Tennessee working with like-minded professionals and business owners from different Latin-American countries. I was observing them and how they did business, and I was able to guide them on business etiquette and expectations. One of the many aspects we addressed was body language. I assure you that researching customary nonverbal aspects are critical, not just for me, but for those that I interact in my personal and professional life. Later on, when developing a Diversity Council for a healthcare system, it was important to have a clear understanding about differences, including genders, regions, religions, and planning. All while respecting unique ways of self-expression and trying to identify ourselves, and how we were perceived by others.

When I moved to Chattanooga and started working for the Chattanooga Area Chamber of Commerce, my cultural lens expanded. Specifically, it was expected of me to focus not only on Latin American business, but absorb an international concept. I had the unique opportunity to develop an international business council composed of 45 countries, 26 languages, and three generations of members. Talk about a rich experience. Once again, body language from every culture was a part of how we communicated. As a result, each monthly meeting highlighted a particular country of focus. Customary business practices, insider details, personal experiences, and cross-cultural challenges made for lively and educational discussions.

At the end of the day, it's not about your particular culture. It is an understanding that we all develop our unique body language to communicate with each other - that it becomes our personal brand.

CHAPTER 7

BELOW THE BELT

In the treasure chest of body language, we often overlook what's going on below the belt. All that is about the change as our minds submerge. We are going to look and dive into the impact that our feet, legs, and hips make through nonverbal communication. While we are intimately knowledgeable of such parts and understand their biological uses, we could better understand how this region of our body talks. There's ample room for misunderstanding as you might imagine.

Simply stated, those two mechanical wonders at the end of our bodies, commonly called feet, tell us where the mind wants to go or what emotion is leaking. Whether our feet are dangling off the edge of our seat, stomping, or wrapped around the legs of a chair, they transmit nonverbal cues to the sharp eye and can display the actual thoughts and feelings from their owner.

A page-turner in the field of anthropology, researchers examined bonobos (remember Kanzi, our 35 year old bonobo from Iowa) and chimpanzees (chimps) in relationship to expressing behaviors through gestures. The researchers coded 43 distinct manual (upper body) and bodily (including feet) gesture signals for both groups. With more than 200 hours of video recordings, they specifically captured 58 hours from bonobos and 146 hours from chimps. Specific to speaking with their bipedal gestures (two feet), they analyzed their swaggers, foot claps, kicks, and stomps. Sounds rather like human behavior to me - or, the latest dance craze. Both groups kicked and stomped, but only the bonobos foot clapped, and only the chimps swaggered. How many chimps do you know who swagger? Don't answer that.

Overall, the experts found that manual and body signals did, in fact, express behaviors and were a distinct part of language. I believe humans are eerily the same. From the stomping feet of a frustrated toddler to the pacing of a nervous groom, our feet communicate. Think about how little you've intentionally observed others' feet beyond their stylish shoes. Be aware, the positioning of the feet is something we could all learn from as a foothold into one's inner thoughts.

As a side note, this same study also gathered data specific to time spent walking, sitting, and lying around. You'd be amazed, or at least amused, how bonobo and chimp time mirrored people. Take a peek:

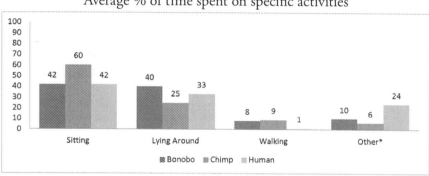

Average % of time spent on specific activities

My thoughts and disclaimer regarding this chart follow. It was difficult to calculate the human factor based on what to measure and specific conditions. Hundreds of surveys calculating human behavior measure different elements and percentages of time spent on activities. Therefore, I read several articles and then did mental averages. Do not consider this chart to be scientific, but rather helpful and eye-opening specific to the parallels of ape and human time and choices. What do you see emerging from the data as a plausible personal action plan? Perhaps, sit less, get busy, walk more, and define exactly how we spend our time other than "Other*." Remember, no matter how swamped you are living your life, we all share the same daily denominator of time. 1,440 minutes. Period.

Now that you are thinking about your feet and even eagerly wiggling them at the thought of how important they are, shift to how we use our feet and legs to communicate with others. I'll provide a few mental images:

Mental image A: Sitting with legs crossed, she gently slips off the heel from her shoe and dangles the foot or shoe back and forth.	Mental image B: A young couple is standing and kissing. One of her feet lifts from the ground like a flamingo.	Mental image C: He slides both of his feet under the chair in a waiting room while preparing for the interview.	Mental image D: Your boss leans back in her office chair, place her legs on the edge of her desk, and crosses her feet at the ankles; exposing the bottom of her shoes to you.

Think about the language coming from these four distinct foot placements. What value, emotion, thought, or belief do you give each situation? Is there only one right answer? Or, could multiple inferences be made depending on the receiver or observer? Here are some possible thoughts and responses for each mental image. Feel free to add your initial thoughts in the blank box at the end of each column after you read each situation.

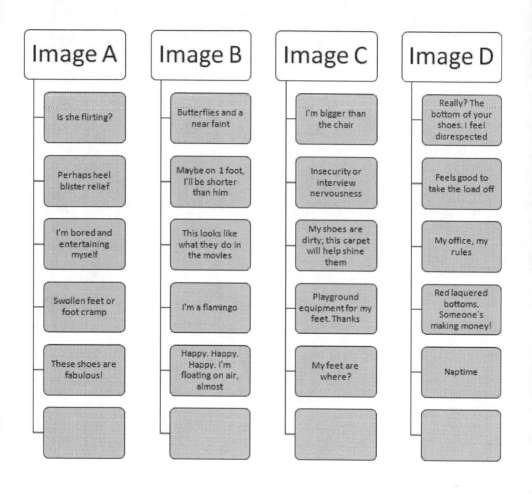

Image A	Image B	Image C	Image D
Is she flirting?	Butterflies and a near faint	I'm bigger than the chair	Really? The bottom of your shoes. I feel disrespected
Perhaps heel blister relief	Maybe on 1 foot, I'll be shorter than him	Insecurity or interview nervousness	Feels good to take the load off
I'm bored and entertaining myself	This looks like what they do in the movies	My shoes are dirty; this carpet will help shine them	My office, my rules
Swollen feet or foot cramp	I'm a flamingo	Playground equipment for my feet. Thanks	Red laquered bottoms. Someone's making money!
These shoes are fabulous!	Happy. Happy. Happy. I'm floating on air, almost	My feet are where?	Naptime

Knowing that there is much to be inferred from our feet and how we use them, think about your choices. Tap one to impress impatience, cross for comfort, and point them in the direction of who interests you or where you want to go.

Moving north, we arrive at the land o' legs. Oh yes, a popular subject for many of us and, all too often, the source of personal and intimate comments, stares, and conversations. Women spend time talking about their own, as well as the condition of others' gams (legs). Men spend time commenting on them as well; and, most of us know this from personal experience. As I mentioned earlier, we spend much of our time focused on the upper part of a body for garnishing nonverbal cues, but time invested to understand how we can enhance our message through our stance, leg crossing, and gait will serve us well.

Stance

Stance is defined as the way we physically posture ourselves to present an attitude. Picture Wonder Woman, the iconic image of Linda Carter dressed in stars and stripes, lasso included, standing ready to protect us. Her arms akimbo and legs planted firmly on the ground, and relatively wide, as if to say, "I dare you to knock me over." You get the picture. We recall this image ever so quickly in part because of her stance. It's wider than an average superhero's off-the-clock posture and done so intentionally. Think about other power images, including world leaders, smaller framed males, single guys portraying big personalities, and classic Western gun fights. Now, focus on their legs and how they stand – imagine John Wayne on the frontier. His feet are shoulder width apart, if not more, and decisive.

Wider leg positions prevail for most of these mental illustrations. We may struggle with this based on the fact that almost all of us were told to stand straight and look like a lady; and, ladies surely don't present wide stances for the world to see. Yet, the data, and most recently, popular videos on YouTube and Ted Talks focused on the influence of Power Posing, have been consuming our data plans. Intentionally positioning our bodies to look like giant "Xs" or Wonder Woman/Super Man, when necessary, shifts others' perceptions, as well as our own our inner thoughts, in terms of power.

Shifting this to work applications, specifically job interviews, researchers studied the nonverbal perceptions of how applicant's stood and for how long, prior to their job interviews or speeches. A series of differently timed positions, high power/low power, were recorded, and participant feedback was included. Researchers studied a host of variables, including speaker awkwardness, body expansion, speaker enthusiasm and confidence, and the ability of the speaker to hold someone's attention. Findings from the speaker's viewpoint found that high power positions solicited feelings of power, being in control, and feeling like a leader. Overall performance was positively impacted. Additionally, feelings of awkwardness were reduced and confidence was boosted. By and large, high power-posed people performed better.

How might we use this information in the workplace? Think about how often you have to present in front of team members? You stand there, papers in hand, power point ablaze, and ready to solve the company's most pressing issues with your brilliant solutions. But, do you look the part of someone confident to lead the project? Perhaps a little power posing prior to your fifteen minutes of fame will make all the difference. Or, think about how you stand with colleagues, particularly men, in the office hallway. Are you physically smaller than them, but want to feel bigger? Slight movements of how we shift our bodies and stance make big impacts.

Adjust your stance. Plant your feet. Literally take a little step and grow you position. I'm not suggesting that you walk into your next staff meeting and stand like Wonder Woman, with cape and wind affects, but stand like you matter. Stand up and be counted. Like a mighty sequoia, portray a sturdy image with your roots firmly fixed to the earth and a bit wider, when necessary, to affirm that no storm or overbearing colleague will damage you. Consider this the next time you have to stand in front of someone or on a team. Conduct yourself professionally and be intentional about how you stand to elicit the image indicative for all you bring to the workplace.

To Sit or To Stand?

That is the question and the answer is - it depends. Some of our work requires that we stand for hours at a time; whereas, other roles require that we sit for hours at our desks. I get a kick out of job descriptions that tell the potential applicant that long hours of standing may be required. What about long hours of sitting? The feeling of entrapment beyond imagination racks our brains after hours of sitting at your desk when, suddenly, a trip to the ladies' room or neighbor's cubicle feels like a full body workout. When we sit for long periods of time at our desks, colleagues remember this and become comfortable walking up to us, exchanging information, and then leaving. How many times did you stop what you were doing, stand up to meet face to face, and have a dialogue? Most likely, not that often. You were busy. You didn't have time to stop what you were doing and reposition your body for a verbal exchange.

Think about it. If the research gives credence to the impact of height and status, why would you remain sitting to converse with someone standing in front of you? Personally, I do not like the view of staring at their pelvic region while conducting business. I would stop, stand, and fully engage with my office guest. I would want her or him to know that I am fully present, stand ready, and have made the effort to position my body for this conversation. Not only is my visitor important, but I am an equal and will ensure that my nonverbals reflect this. I have witnessed too many situations in which the person in power, perhaps the supervisor, manager, or division director, physically towers over their "subjects," I mean team members, like a king addressing their serfs. While this may be a bit extreme, consider the perception of who's in charge. And, who are the dutiful students in that team planning session?

When the situation calls for it, decide if you want to stand or sit. Just because a chair is offered, does not necessarily mean you want to take it. Savvy professionals know when to pull up a chair for a hard conversation in that it might lessen the bad news. Confident leaders are aware of their decision to sit or stand as the need arises to either give company directives or let the team know that we're on equal ground. As you learn about your intentional use of sit and stand time based on situation and degree of impact, remember to make a conscious effort for how you want others to perceive you. No wallflowers allowed.

One healthcare study asked 120 adult patients to rate the time that their provider spent at their bedside, either standing or sitting, in relationship to patient satisfaction and perceived positive provider-patient rapport. They concluded that, when caregivers sat bedside, patients perceived a more positive interaction then when the healthcare professional stood to deliver care. Patients felt that their physician even spent more time with them, though this was not the case, when they sat with them. Their perceptions of feeling comforted were addressed by the intentional action of knowing when to sit or when to stand.

Walking on, I mean, moving on. As we add to our toolbox of deliberately deciding how we want to be perceived and received by others, a focus on how we sit, in particular, in front of other people, is quite important. As women, we are acutely aware of how a man sits in front of us, with open legs, and a wide display of the crotch at times. What exactly does this mean? Is he incapable of crossing his legs? Does he have a chafing issue? Most likely, no. This wide display is for public viewing and often exhibited by young, healthy males as a way of saying "Look at me. All of me. I am healthy." This chair consuming position emits a strong nonverbal statement – and usually not positive from many of the women in the room. We typically have no interest in his 'look at me, I'm healthy' status.

Now, picture a group of women sitting with wide displays. Not too pretty. I need not say more because we, as women, rarely sit this way. But, give some time as to how we adjust our bodies while seated. Do we sit with knees and feet clamped together like demure, modest school girls or do we hoist one leg over the other while engaging in a healthy conversation? For some, bending the knees and wrapping the feet around the chair legs sounds inviting. For others, this gymnastic activity might produce a foot cramp. Lest we forget that flexible colleague who can sit for hours with her foot curled under her buttocks without the slightest notice.

At the workplace and amongst mixed gender company, how we sit and position our bodies speaks to others. The legwork of how we work our legs can either support our verbal message, or diminish it. If you choose to sit while conducting business, then consider how you look while sitting. I pose a few questions to ponder:

- Do you sit erect or slouch in your chair?

- Like the three little bears, how big are you in comparison to the size of such chair?

- If there are arms on this chair, do you use them or keep your wenises near your torso?

- Do you decide to cross your leg right over left, or left or right; and does it even matter?

- How about an ankle cross? Not so much effort, but still a modest position.

- Finally, if you decide to cross your legs at the knees, what exactly is the view for others up your thigh while wearing a skirt or dress?

While these questions are posed with a light touch, the business of sitting is serious. A study of more than 1,200 people looked at a variety of factors and the issue of occupational and leisure sitting time. They collected a wealth of information on socio-demographic attributes, gender, physical activity, weight/height, and high/low occupational sitting time vs. TV viewing time (leisure). Several correlations were made between age, marital status, seat time at work, type of work or occupation, income level, and impact on health. All attributes, but higher BMI in men and energy consumption for women, were factors in high occupational sitting time. The researchers did suggest that sit time reduction strategies, particularly for women, are important and should be considered at the workplace.

For us, that may mean that women who sit at work for the majority of their days are negatively impacted in terms of health, type of job, and income; let alone, the perceptions of perceived power or submission. For this reason, I share with you Mile's Law, "Where you stand depends on where you sit." Powerful, isn't it? I heard another witty one the other day that basically said, "You're either at the table, or on the menu." While these cleverly written words are simple in verbiage, they provide a wealth of information for anyone wanting to understand their value. Make sure you are at the table, sitting there because you <u>know</u> you belong.

Ideas to Consider:

1. If you have a say in how your office furniture is arranged, think about how you want to be perceived while sitting there conducting your business. Make sure your back isn't to the door. Literally; it may send the wrong, negative message. Feng shui away.

2. Ponder the purpose of your meetings or conferences. Decide whether it is appropriate and beneficial to sit or stand.

3. As we take in the whole person when reading body language, consider how your shoes match, or don't match your image. Dirty soles may have some thinking, dirty person.

4. When you sit in a meeting, make sure you utilize the arms on the chair to your advantage. Need to feel noticed or a little emotionally bigger, extend your elbows (both of them) to rest atop of those padded, leather chair arms.

<u>Take-away:</u>

Your feet and how you stand impacts power and perception. Remember, high power-posed people perform better.

CARBON INTO DIAMONDS	
Reflections ... *What I gleaned from this chapter*	Personal Action Plan ... *What I plan to do with this new knowledge*

IDIOM EPISODE #7

The team just left the office after a long day of hearing the details of the new strategic plan. Each person has been assigned a piece of the project and each has an opinion.

designed by freepik.com

Sage Story

Common Sense by Rachel Slikker

Even in this day and age, as a woman, I still have to work hard to be taken seriously in the workplace; yet I don't want to lose my unique feminine contribution. The best way to do this is to be mindful and to be prepared. I have to be mindful of what image I'm projecting, mindful of what words I use to communicate, and mindful of my own emotions. All while preparing for scheduled meetings and chance encounters.

I manage the Tennessee Career Center which means I interact with a wide range of employers and a unique community of job seekers. The biggest eye-opener has been that other people don't think like me. You might think, "Well, duh, Rachel." But, the truth is that each of us has knowledge we consider "common sense" or "common knowledge" because we have always known it. This does not mean everyone else knows it. For example, don't let your behind hang out the top of your jeans, or show cleavage when job searching or while at work. It turns out, not everyone is aware of this.

At the Career Center, I have witnessed a girl in a bikini top and cut-off shorts applying for a job. Sure, the application is online, but we have employers in our building daily who are interviewing on the spot. Obviously, she was not ready. I also have met with people who I suspected were under the influence of alcohol or had not made good hygiene choices that morning. The truth is, whether you are going to the Career Center, the grocery store, or post office, you never know who you will bump into. You might meet someone on aisle 9 who can help your career. But those examples are pretty obvious.

There are numerous subtleties of inappropriateness including showing too much leg or cleavage or wearing clothes that are too tight. I have to be careful when I buy a dress, because I am tall and a dress that looks good on my shorter friends, on me looks like I'm clubbing. As in WAY too short. I also keep a scarf on hand in case I have more showing than I intended. I want to be pretty, but professional. My job with my customers is to educate them on what potential employers see and want. The best assistance I can provide others is not a new resume or interviewing tips (although those are important). The best I offer is a dose of "common sense" for dressing appropriately, responsibly, and meeting and exceeding expectations in the workplace.

I am also mindful of the words I use in that they are clear and concise. I once had a coworker who would always speak in meetings, but she had a hard time being clear and concise. She was not good at articulating and would become flustered. She also used malapropos such as kiosh instead of kiosk, and swavy when she meant savvy. I saw firsthand how this affected her credibility with her co-workers and partners.

It is not possible to always be 100% prepared, but I can do my best. If I'm going into a management meeting, I consciously choose a couple of things I want to mention. I don't wait to be called upon, but I do wait until it is appropriate to speak. I keep up-to-date on enrollment numbers and which employers are using our services. This is my contribution to the discussion. Speaking up in meetings is imperative for my career and to be seen as someone who adds value. I listen and observe, then I contribute. I learned this through much practice because I had a reputation for blurting out whatever came to mind and embarrassing myself.

As a leader, I continuously try to improve my communication with the people I supervise. I had a boss who was difficult to work for because she often made spur-of-the-moment decisions based on her trigger emotions. Those decisions were usually communicated with a healthy dose of sarcasm. As I moved into a leadership role, I decided that I would not make decisions based on my emotions. I would not talk down to the people I supervised. What I have noticed from this choice is better decision-making and a more loyal staff. Nobody likes to be spoken to like a child. If I have done something wrong, I would appreciate feedback and I'll own my mistakes all day long. I do not, however, appreciate being spoken to as though I am a moron. This method fails to produce good results. I know that my staff feels the same way.

We all make mistakes, but the people around us will take advice much better when given with some kindness, humor, and humility. It is easy to focus on others' errors and correcting them, however, it is just as important to give my staff validation when they do the right thing. I have found that this above all else (whether it be perks, raises, days off, etc.) is one of the best motivators for people. If I want to be successful reaching my goals, my team needs to be successful. The best way to influence that outcome, I have found, is to motivate those who help me reach my goals.

To do a good job in life, whether it be work, home, dating, friends, traveling, etc. I have to understand that I have something important to contribute, but also, that every person I meet, young and old, have something to teach me. I want to remember that everyone I meet knows something that I don't know. I want to continue to add to my knowledge and understanding of the world around me in order to become a better me.

CHAPTER 8

THE TORSO

Typically, we see this part of our body when we enter a business office and greet the person at the front desk, sit around a table and chat about something, or view people on TV when the camera scans the crowd. Our torso. A canvas of arms, legs, and head colliding and, simultaneously, packed with important organs like our hearts and stomachs. In the realm of nonverbal communication, this relatively colossal part of our physical being has much to say when arriving for conversation.

Growing up, and quickly I might add in the height department, my mother would always tell me to stand up straight. As an adolescent of Amazonian size, in my mind, that would only make me taller. This fourteen year old felt zero desire to suck it in, pull it back, and waltz into the world with carriage held high. However, I now see the ramifications of failing to do this all around me. Hunched shoulders, arched backs, and seemingly downtrodden souls moving silently around me with the air knocked out of their sails. Ok, so that's a little dramatic, but really, look around. It's rare to see people, and all too often women, moving about with correct and erect posture. We slouch. We tilt. We slide. I have a hunch that we hunch too much. All around us we see people with a meek outside image which, in fact, may communicate the wrong message given all that is big and significant within us.

Whether sitting or standing, posture is important. As a 6'3" woman with heels on, I am proud to say that on more than one occasion, someone has come up to me and complimented me on my excellent posture. My parents are so proud. Research also confirms the idea that how we sit and stand matter for not only good health, but for perceptions.

Framing their work around the perceptions of emotion, experts understand that we associate body postures with emotions, particularly when facial elements are involved. We're quite good, starting in childhood. One study asked participants, both children and adults, to consider a scenario and then look at photographs to identify emotions. The researcher used the possible feelings of fear, sadness, happiness, and anger; and they provided faces showing these emotions. Separate corresponding body poses with the same emotions were also used. Participants then had to identify the face with the body to match the emotion. With great accuracy, both children and adults were able to match the photographs. This study suggested that, when we look at someone's face displaying an emotion, we are influenced by the body position as well.

Take this to the office setting. Look around; how are colleagues standing while talking with other people? What do they look like while sitting at their desks? Do their bodies match their facial expressions? With many of today's trendy glass-walled offices, it's quite a landscape for capturing emotions without anyone uttering a word. A great study in the *Psychology of Women Quarterly* offered another reason for women to sit up, stand up, and be counted. Eighty female participants were asked to complete a series of tasks from both upright and slouched positions, seated in a child's chair or powerful throne, all while wearing either a formfitting tank top or loose sweatshirt. They found that posture not only impacted moods and feelings, but even possibly the perceptions of our relationship with power and status. I think I'll leave the power sweatshirt suit at home though.

Back to taking heed with Mom's advice. I'm standing tall. I'm walking the walk, and talking the talk. As a part of standing erect, I know that our bodies shift from side to side while walking and standing due to the powerful hip structure known as our pelvis. The second largest bone in the human body, this structure connects the lower part of us with our torso and is, for some eager to have children, the cradle of life. For others, it's what rests within our padded bottoms and, for a few, the reason we cringe at the thought of the phrase, the pelvic girdle. I'll call it our hips.

Irrespective of what we call it, women tend to have extreme control over this region of their bodies. From the time we hit puberty, this area begins to noticeably change and for the average shaped female, an hourglass silhouette begins to appear. Hips also play a role in gender identification, the fit our clothing, a wide range of commentaries, and how we, as women, decide when and if we want our hips to talk.

A fertile hotbed for gender-based comments, many workplace environments are ripe for a discussion about gender, discrimination, and even bullying. We know all three exist and, to whatever degree, personally and professionally, impact us. Experts point-out that, when the behavior of women deviates from traditional roles, they tend to be negatively evaluated. In turn, workplace bullying, from in-your-face comments to more subtle overtones, often results.

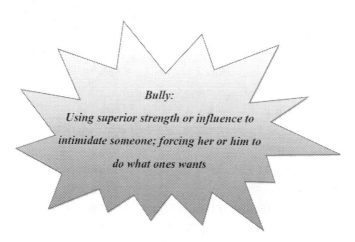

Bully:

Using superior strength or influence to intimidate someone; forcing her or him to do what ones wants

Gender-focused research, both internationally and in our own backyards, confirm that women "are easier targets" in the workplace and both genders experience different types of bullying. Given a host of interpersonal management and communication styles, the perception of even being bullied is received differently. For example, your supervisor may have no issues with "innocent" name-calling and mild, sarcastic threats of getting fired as a way of joking. But you, receiver of such information feel rattled, trapped, and perceive few options. You begin to emotionally erode. It's my job. What will I do? How can he say that? Who can I tell? Will they believe me? Am I overreacting? He's golfing friends with the owner. The scripts of self-doubt begin to flourish as our production levels dive. Help.

Practical advice, based in research and approved from this woman's perspective, suggests that we, as professionals, leaders, and women, actively practice proactive and response techniques.

Promote a Positive Work Culture

Hold yourself accountable from whatever desk you control. Create or help with initiatives that establish clear-cut policies when bullying occurs for both genders. Action is swift. Acknowledge that there are two genders and call it straight. This whole notion of not noticing genders is a myth. We notice. Both genders also report negative effects on mental and physical health. Whereas a slightly stronger connection between negative acts and health effects were higher for women, both men and women perceived these bullying experiences differently. Take note of who is investigating the complaint. Their bias may play a role in interpreting the facts and resolution.

Enlist Top Management

With the support of high level decision makers, a zero tolerance anti-bullying policy stands a chance of becoming the standard when high level decision makers are professionally invested with the issue. Figure out if the leaders who inspire you, and show excitement to have you on their teams, practice ethical and professional behavior without even thinking about it. Sharp ears will quickly pick-up whispers of wife bashing, incessant partner complaining, or off-colored stories when gender is the main character. You do not want to be a part of this team.

Follow the Trail

References and on-boarding processes should clearly establish how men and women conduct themselves and, when a violation occurs, victims should be encouraged to come forward without fear of retribution. Fear is one of our most powerful emotions and, often, dictates what we will and will not do. Any company that operates from fear will eventually crush its most valuable resource.

Be Aware

Sometimes people say things without really listening to themselves. Provide opportunities, and if possible, formal trainings, to help employees understand actions driving bad behaviors and the consequences connected with such habits. Ask people for feedback and get their perspectives on situations. Sometimes a confidential survey may be the perfect way to give a victim a voice. Make sure that the results from the data are placed in the right hands: the ethical, empathetic, action-driven decision makers who know how to get things done. Everyone hates to waste their time taking surveys at work that go nowhere. That's just a waste of time for everyone and changes nothing.

Control You

Whatever you decide to do, or not to do, remember that you have control over one thing. **You.** You can decide to take a stand, or sit this one out. Being fully engaged and participating at the workplace means that you have to determine your personal ROI (return on investment). Questions about your investments and sacrifices will play out through your body (also known as leaks); so, make peace with your brain and what rattles around. If you know that your value system is being challenged, this will eventually make you: 1. Glow like a worm, or 2. Wither away. We must be fed and our colleagues, friends, and family have the ability to nourish or starve us; particularly as women.

In turn, I offer a mound of information to add to your full plate. Decide what you'd like to eat.

Ideas to Consider:

1. Remember the words of Columbian singer, Shakira, in that the "hips don't lie." As you perfect your stance, sitting, and placement of legs, all convene at the massive bone structure connecting our upper and lower bodies. Be aware of this potent part of your body as you walk, sit, and saunter through life.

2. Bullying is serious business. While it's a lesson in most school classrooms, adults who practice these behaviors should be checked. Look for people who mirror your inner values and shine with them.

3. Stand erect with the body you've been given. Things that go 'up' tend to do better. Grow, seek something greater than yourself, and ensure that your body is being intellectually, emotionally, and physically cultivated.

4. People watch. Observe your workplace and learn the interpersonal and intrapersonal dynamics between colleagues. You will be provided with an epic amount of information without necessarily speaking with anyone. Harvest the nuggets from your hard work.

<u>Take-Away:</u>

Be the leader against sexist or discriminatory workplaces. As a powerful woman, have a personal *zero-tolerance mindset*. Ensure that you stand up (with great posture) and be heard - then sit down.

CARBON INTO DIAMONDS	
Reflections ... *What I gleaned from* *this chapter*	Personal Action Plan ... *What I plan to do with* *this new knowledge*

IDIOM EPISODE #8

Renee, Richard, and Andrew are in charge of the logistics and limited budget for executing the annual conference. With more questions than answers, the team is considering all options.

Sage Story

You Make the Magic Happen by Brittany Gray

Where I come from, you don't allow the small stuff to affect you. Let's be honest, only a few of us were made to really LIVE this way. This story is for the ladies who are fearless, genuine, and live their truths. In my experience, this has been the route to discovery and freedom (mostly from myself). The biggest truth of living in your truth is the good it does for others. You never know who is watching you, expecting you to "drop the ball," or lose all of your marbles. Most of the time, it's you, who is your biggest enemy and doubter. Yes, you! Let me explain how I overcame this hurdle.

I wasn't always the poised or resilient human being I see in the mirror each and every morning I wake-up. There were times when I was challenged personally and, oh boy, did I have some decisions to make professionally. As a proud Crohnie and Alopecian, I found out real quick that life isn't always that pretty. It's what you make it. I'm often surprised when people comment on my hair and its diversity of style; or the shade or fit of dress I decide to wear on any given day. For most it's amazement, and praise, for my capacity to push through and show-up. But for others, it's a blessing and a curse. How is it that we keep "it" all together and seem to be just "fine?" At this point, it's important to observe and bear witness to your environment - this is when it gets interesting.

At this point in time, you may not be sure how your information was received, but realize that your communication and messaging (verbal and non-verbal), shared through your movement, appearance, and gestures, are points of interest. This is when things can be taken out of context, or you may notice a change in how others see you in particular settings. Your confidence and awareness of self are often mistaken for negative traits of grandeur or narcissism. Let's not forget to mention that this situation is often elevated by other factors such as age, experience, level of competence, and hierarchy. If you are able to stay abreast and in tune to what is occurring around you, there's a chance you pick up on it.

I'm thankful for the few women who support and contribute to my development that help me decipher between healthy and unhealthy. As a young woman starting her career, or a woman starting over with renewed purpose, you carry with you a gift. You possess a sense of purity and joy that is contagious, but rarely present in some contexts. This truth can present individuals with situations that are not always conducive to this optimal mindset. You may experience verbal or emotional attacks or hurtful experiences when your intentions, beliefs, dress, or style are misread and received poorly.

So, I offer you one solution: own it. There are in-exchangeable value-adds that you were meant to embody. Growth in spirit and growth in mindset are two core contributors to our daily responses, actions, and behaviors. It is not our destiny or responsibility to remain stagnant or sour because of the cards we were dealt. When I realized the power of my impact upon others, my only responsibility in my personal and professional life shifted to fulfilling my journey as a conduit for change. Mere presence and energy can heal brokenness and infuse confidence into sunken atmospheres. However, this only occurs when you are able to monitor and manage your internal feelings, emit the best of yourself, and all its glory. Life is that much easier and richer for those around you. I forever believe in the power of you, your journey, and the people who become better because of it. This is how we heal the world! It's not a mantra. It's not an idea. It's a way of being. You have the ability to pick-up your pieces. You make magic happen, baby! This is how I empower ME as a result the women surrounding me.

CHAPTER 9

CLOTHING MATTERS

Kick up your heels! I wear a women's size 12. I hear your gasps, catch your downward glance, and watch your eyebrows elevate - followed by the classic question, "Where on earth do you buy your shoes?" Well, at the canoe store, of course! Kidding aside, a young woman with a size 12 in the 1980s was challenged to find footwear that wasn't: 1. A man's shoe in a size 10; or 2. An orthotic soft-soled white or black masterpiece designed to drag me into the Golden years - with arch support. In both cases, this woman did not relish the thought of shoe shopping. That, needless to say, has changed as I scan my near hundred pairs of heels, in all colors, materials, and heights, lining my closet shelves.

By Freepik.com

But, there's an interesting thing about shoes; in particular, women's heels. A fascinating heel height study found that "men's helping behavior increased as soon as heel length increased." What! Am I actually typing that the higher the heel, the more a man will help me? So it seems. Let me explain how this was found to carry truth based on the research. Four back-to-back studies were conducted in which a woman was placed in a situation, wore heels of different heights, and performed simple tasks under different conditions. The findings were intriguing. When women wore higher heel heights, men responded more favorably. From the time it took a man to make eye contact and then approach a single, seated female in a bar to helping retrieve a dropped glove while walking along a city street, the outcomes were consistent. Men were quicker to respond, help, talk with, and comply when the woman wore a high heel. Interestingly though, woman to woman encounters did not solicit the same behaviors and reactions.

So, while I am not telling you to purchase a pair of stilettos and saunter the halls of the office, I am suggesting that you consider your professional attire from head to toe, literally. Invest your time and money in shoes that flatter your feet, empower you, fit well, and reflect your professional image. Consider this an investment in your wardrobe worthy of time and attention.

While I'd like to believe that flip flops (those wonderful foam beach shoes in a rainbow of colors) do not impact others' impressions of me, I do know that wearing them in a professional setting will produce negative perceptions of me from those I want to build relationships with specific to my workplace. At the same time, just wearing the same old heel-damaged shoes might say that I do not have attention to detail which, as I believe each of us can attest, is far from the truth.

As we continue our journey on clothing, women, and the workplace, again, the research is impressive and I do not mean the "research" from drugstore style magazine surveys asking you to pick Dress A or Dress B. Research confirms that women show more skin at work. This makes sense when we think of skirt lengths, short sleeves, and dipping necklines. One study found that women display at least 17% more skin than our male counterparts. Eek. 17%! Compare that to a man's suit in which we can only see two parts – his face and his hands. The rest of him is completely covered; therefore, our eyes can only focus on what his face and the message coming from it. And, as we agree, skin is the largest living organ, sensitive, and, at times, quite sensual to the touch. I believe I don't want just anyone's eyes looking at my displayed sensitive, living organ at the workplace, thank you very much!

When I see a female at the office, like most of you, I take in the length of her skirt, the plunge of her blouse, the fit of the clothing, and how she carries herself - in just a few seconds. It doesn't take long to absorb the image. Unlike a covered man, I cannot just focus on her face and hands; there's just too much to look at on her canvas. Sadly, and way too often, I see my incredibly intelligent and gifted colleagues wearing short-short skirts which beg the question of sitting and exposure, plunging necklines beckoning my eyes to greet "the girls," and not so subtle tugging and pulling to realign clothing one size too small.

You get the picture. We see it all around us every day and the good news is that we, as women, can help each other. From gentle suggestions to affirming comments when something goes right, let's help each other with the rules of wardrobes and settings. Thousands of online articles, blogs, and helpful hints offer practical, affordable, and reasonable suggestions for both men and women of all shapes and sizes to make positive and lasting impressions. One helpful piece of advice I learned pertains to cleavage. I know, that wonderfully dreadful and excitingly mystical part of every woman's body. Breasts. From large to small, perky to not so much, breast-talk has long been a part of world cultures, locker rooms, and bedroom scenes. It goes without saying, though I will now officially say, breasts are talked about at the workplace. What? "How dare them!" "That's personal!" "It's none of their business!" Exactly. Your breasts (and my breasts, too) are off the table for workplace viewing, ogling, staring, brushing past, and water cooler conversations.

However, this is often not the case. We see them proudly, and not so proudly, displayed at the office. Workplace landscapes of all shapes and sizes are ladled with mountains of necklines deeper than oceans and blouses tighter than dolphin skin. From ready-to-burst buttons to the classic shivering nipples, breasts consume workplace spaces. What are our colleagues' eyes supposed to do given these conditions? Look. Yes. Advice.

Not really. We could only hope a concerned team member would help us avoid these social nightmares, but reality dictates otherwise. Frank discussions about this area bring up horrific images of possible sexual harassment. Let's face it; most adults in our building would rather head off to an un-medicated root canal than be subjected to this subject.

Help is on the way, though, if you happen to: 1. Possess such described breasts, or 2. Been subject to visual images seared in your brain from someone at the office displaying such described breasts. The professional woman understands the basics of clothing, fit, foundation, and conscience. Invest time to find a good fitting bra and then buy several. Remember that padding helps when the office thermostat takes a dive. It is hard to be portrayed as a professional of equal status when one's nipples are erect and part of the team.

Next, think about size. Do our blouses fit and complement our shape and size? It's one thing to wear a stretchy pullover top, but when buttons are involved, you must confirm that no button will provide a peep show for the person standing next to you. I can guarantee that a beautiful pink lacy bra in partial view will trump any professional discussions about finalizing contracts or investing in the next big deal. That bra is the next big deal. As for the topic of cleavage and exposed skin, men are masters of this.

Think about a man's suit - you only see his face and his hands. On women, the chest skin is often available for viewing. For that reason, you get to decide just how much you want to show. I recommend a simple rule that involves your hand as your measure. Roughly 5" down from the bottom of your neck is considered a conservative plunge for exposed skin and acceptable at the workplace. There is no need to grab a tape measure and permanently tattoo an acceptable neckline; however, understand what people see when they look at you and maintain absolute control as to what you will allow them to see.

While we are intellectual equals, our bodies are different. We have curves and body parts that are special to every female body. Embrace this and also learn the techniques that enhance and flatter all you bring to your work and social interactions. Some people spend thousands of dollars to understand these techniques. Candid conversations from experienced women and those who have your best interest may provide similar advice for a little of their time and a latte.

For example, did you know that men have this technique specific to their belts, watchbands, and shoes? Somewhere during those awkward growing years, a well-dressed professional learned that these artifacts should match in both color and material. A brown belt should naturally complement brown leather loafers and snazzy brown leather watchbands. Talk about tying the details together.

Speaking of color, the multi-billion dollar industry of color palettes also impacts us in the workplace. One study examined the positive effects of color, status, judgment of others, and perceptions of self. Photos of participants wearing six different colored tops (same style) were presented to female and male raters. The findings were significant for some of the colors of choice and the feelings they provoked. This held true for both genders and results found that clothing color impacted our perceptions and behaviors. Without diving into statistical significance and confidence integrals, it's safe to say that the colors we wear matter. There just might be some science as to why basic black and power red envelop us at work.

As you begin to look at the hues and colors of your own body palette, learn how your colors enrich or harm your professional, and personal, image. While that trendy, silky blouse is perfect for a weekend party, how that same blouse may be perceived at the workplace is quite the opposite. This mindset holds steady from top to bottom! Think about how we look at other people, knowing that, all too often, we hold women to a different standard in our society. Do we compliment her when something looks fantastic? Do we feel threatened that her workplace attire draws attention? Are we quick to point-out her flaws compared to what's working for her image?

Several studies about women, clothing, and the workplace yielded similar results and made lasting impressions, particularly if the impressions were negative. I'll highlight a few; again, to demonstrate the fact that we talk with our bodies and what we put on them.

- Women have to work harder to create a good impression

- Women are more likely to be judged on appearance

- Clothing choices, even the most subtle ones, strongly influence others in terms of confidence, success, flexibility, and salary level

- Particularly in management and executive level positions, women would be wise to pay extra attention to their clothing choices

Finally, a study involving 90 employed women and 54 female college students participated in a study about first impressions at the workplace. All were solicited from social media, including Facebook and LinkedIn. Photos for rating included females wearing more provocative or less provocative clothing and a higher or lower status label. The high status job was a 'senior manager' and the low status was a 'receptionist.' The findings, as you already imagined, found that provocative clothing equaled lower status perceptions. Furthermore, high status females were judged harsher when their clothing was more provocative. Erring on the side of conservative may benefit us as we move-up professional spaces and make positive, lasting impressions from our fellow employees and those we want to impress.

Women are notorious for harming each other. I, for the most part, chalk this up to biology and natural selection. However, it does not have to be this way. The best, most resilient survive and the competition is tough. If both males and females in the human and animal world fail to adapt, adjust, and garner attention, over time, poor outcomes could result. Apply this rationale to women and men at work. It's hard to get ahead when someone else wants it more and works harder for it. How many times have you put your best foot forward only to be passed-up by someone putting their foot through the door first? How do you ensure that your image beams in a room full of sunshine? The bottom line, be the change you want to see … in your workplace. What will _you_ do to not harm, but help, another woman?

Here are a few questions to consider when examining your current wardrobe, your workplace favorites, and what you might need going forward to enhance you!

- ☐ How much of your body is exposed? Are you drawing someone's eyes to where you want them to focus?

- ☐ Does it really matter if we wear a 12, 14, or 16? Or, a 4 versus a 2. A 14 or 20? It's a number, people. Just that. I know this well. I wear a 12. At times, a 14. Other times, a 10.

- ☐ Do I want to invest in a few higher priced, well-fitting pieces of professional clothing that stand the test of time, or am I budgeting for volume and trendiness?

☐ What types of fabrics and cuts are best for my shape and size? Clothiers make junior, women, and plus for a reason. They also make petite, average, and tall.

While I like to think that "mirror, mirror, on the wall" reflects exactly what I believe is true, perceptions of self and others crack that prophecy. Though I detest some of the labels thrust upon us, like a size 12 referenced as a plus size, I have zero control over changing those labels. I prefer we take those words and make them sound something magnificent like, "I am a *junior* executive *woman* at the office; *plus,* an awesome member of my team."

What I do have absolute control over, though, is how I chose to dress my body from head to toe every single day. I also have control how I treat others in the workplace. Be supportive, like a good underwire.

Ideas to Consider:

1. Since the birthday suit of nudity isn't an option for any workplace I know of or frequent, you have to put something on yourself. Know that while you are covering inches of skin, you are painting a canvas with your choices. **Make your work of art priceless**.

2. Though your checkbook may reflect your financial inability to purchase the latest Italian fashions, do not worry. Clothing in our country is abundant. Higher-end resale shops, from boutique to big box, offer new and gently used name brands with bargain price tags to build your personal brand.

3. As women, the gift of our breasts should not be treated any less. No matter your size or age, take time to find what works for your shoulders, back meat, and cup size. Make this foundational piece part of you, especially since you'll be wearing it for up to 18 hours, as the advertisers tell us.

4. Take notice of women in your world. A well-timed, genuine compliment coming from a woman carries substantial weight. In a society driven by punishment and with childhood scripts

of bad vs. good judgments, make the effort to be the good in a woman's life. As you help her glow, you will also reap the benefits of practicing how you want to be treated.

<u>Take-Away:</u>

Select an ensemble that exudes confidence and intelligence while also complementing your body type.

CARBON INTO DIAMONDS	
Reflections ... *What I gleaned from this chapter*	Personal Action Plan ... *What I plan to do with this new knowledge*

IDIOM EPISODE #9

In the Executive lounge, the power players converse over the recent release of the Shareholder's Report. Should we go public? Did we get that VP from the competition?

Sage Story

My "Mom-Uniform" by Marianne Lorren

When I think about traditional uniforms, what comes to mind are military uniforms, school uniforms, fast food uniforms, nursing scrubs, or mechanic's shirts with name badges. Our ways of dressing signal to others who we are, where we are supposed to be, our status, expected behaviors, and what body of knowledge we possess. Throughout my working years, I have had many roles that required a uniform. As a teenager working at a grocery store, I remember zipping up my required brown and orange polyester smock. During college, I wore the mandatory white uniform and hairnet for my job in a food manufacturing plant. As a society, we are comfortable with uniforms.

Perhaps without realizing it, we all wear uniforms every day. I stayed home with my three children before they entered elementary school. I joked with my mom friends about the "mom-uniform;" some variation of stretchy yoga pants or jeans with an absorbent t-shirt or tank top, hair back in a ponytail — purely practical. At baby play-dates, we all showed up in the mom-uniform, with sneakers or flip-flops. The uniforms we wear signal to others that we belong in a group. I can still spot the mom-uniform at the park or grocery store.

I re-entered the paid work force about two years ago. It was a huge transition for me! During Christmas break, I was driving kids around in my totally cool mini-van; two weeks later I was working 55 hours a week in a busy professional firm. I wanted to be successful and gain the respect of my new employer. But, after toting three small children around for a decade in my yoga pants and sneakers, how could I fit into my new environment?

Physical appearance and attire communicate much about an individual. What did I want to communicate? I looked around me for cues. In the media, a successful woman's body, clothing, and hairstyle are scrutinized, debated, and seem to eclipse discussions of her professional accomplishments. My professional worth is a combination of my education, experience and judgment. Yet, in our society, there is an emphasis on outward appearance as a gauge of success.

How can I operate in a system that evaluates my intelligence and professional competence, particularly because I am a woman, by how I dress and adorn myself? Why the constant public discussion of how, or if, a woman can do it all: success at work, a well-adjusted family, a smoothly running household, all while also looking beautiful to maintain the interest of her romantic partner? I am keenly aware of the constant assessment of my external appearance as proof that I "have it all together" and can "do it all," even as I chafe at the unfairness. To be successful, I am expected to look and dress the parts I play — to wear the uniform.

Each morning I gaze at the sea of conventional black, navy, and gray suits with boring long sleeved button-up shirts that now inhabit my closet. It's not what I love wearing; it's not who I am. But I consider the traditional attire as just another work uniform and an investment in myself. It's not what most of the females in my office wear. I dress more like the men. My work clothing and accessories are conservative because I want the focus to be squarely on my ideas and accomplishments.

My work attire is selected to echo that of the top leadership of my firm; even though that is not where I am now. My clients are not interested in my fun side or expression of my individuality. The focus must be on them and their needs, not on my tugging down a short skirt or adjusting straps under a sheer blouse.

I don't need to sway around on 4" heels and wear a tight pencil skirt to be a beautiful and feminine woman. I want to make it easy for my boss to pay attention to my work, not my physique. My focus is on providing excellent client service and a respectful work environment — respectful of myself and of others. My work uniform helps me accomplish that.

When I get home, I shed the expectations of my work day along with my suit, and put on my comfortable, non-glamorous mom-uniform. Yet, one day last summer, as I was picking up my kids from day camp in my business uniform, one of my daughter's new friends looked at me with round eyes and whispered, "Is your mom a movie star?" Why yes, yes I am.

CHAPTER 10

WRAP THIS UP - FOR NOW

This chapter is about reminding, not rehashing, everything we covered between the covers. There's a great deal to digest as you reflect, practice, fail, get back up, and dust yourself off. You are a phenomenal professional, whether raw or mature, who brings a wealth of assets to the office the second you walk through the door. Embrace yourself and hold your head high (but not too high – that'll look like arrogance.)

9 Ways Woman Win with Body Language
Take-Aways

#1 – **Enrich your spoken vocabulary through selective word choice, conversation starters, and articulation. Monitor your social media reputation.**

#2 – **A personal sound check may be in order. People hear almost all of your sounds and sighs. These sounds speak loudly about your inner feelings and thoughts, and impact your outward behaviors.**

#3 – **Female and male brains are different. Embrace the variety because both have value in the workplace. The simple necessity for positive leadership: Listen.**

#4 – Body image is still a fight. Take a step in your personal and professional world to shatter the negative images in the mirror and see the carats of diamonds. Even with your flaws, you are priceless.

#5 – Face it. The face matters and so does its crowning glory. Make educated decisions about both. As you promote women, know that your feminism philosophy fights for all that is equal to that of men; and we can advocate while wearing a bit of mascara.

#6 – Your handshake is an extension of you – make it a good one. Check your gestures to ensure that they convey their intended meanings.

#7 – Your feet and how you stand impacts power and perception. Remember, high power-posed people perform better.

#8 – Be the leader against sexist or discriminatory workplaces. As a powerful woman, have a personal *zero-tolerance mindset*. Ensure that you stand up (with great posture) and be heard - then sit down.

#9 – Select an ensemble that exudes confidence and intelligence while also complementing your body type.

Because it's fun to see what we learned, below is a self-assessment quiz to determine if you are ready to speak the nonverbal language required for your workplace and social life. Good luck, though I suspect you'll do very well in that you reflected and acted to each diamond extracted from the carbon landscape.

1. What does the Fe in Female stand for?

2. What is the 7/28/55 rule?

3. Is there an optimal rate per minute when talking? If so, what is it?

4. What does LISTEN stand for regarding active listening?

5. When pondering your own body language, remember to _____ the possibilities, _____ in your wrinkles, treasure comes in all _____ and _____. And, always see the _____ in your mirror!

6. Even with our flaws, what precious stone are we?

7. How fast do we make a first impression?

8. Eyeglasses were first made in _____.

9. Remember, feminists can wear _____.

10. The simple formula for an effective smile is to contract your _____ along with your _____.

11. What should connect/touch/hook in a solid handshake?

12. Your handshake is an _____ of you.

13. What forms the base of your power stance?

14. Before a meeting, decide whether you'll _____ or _____.

15. Turn life's carbon into _____.

16. You have control over one thing: _____.

17. The body never _____.

18. What is the largest organ?

19. Strong women can be like a good _____ for one another – supportive and uplifting.

20. Tap the _____ _____ of your life to create a menagerie of glistening _____!

I did not provide an answer key to this quiz because you don't need one. You are smart and the answers are herein.

Attempting to figure out how to end this book has been the most difficult part of writing it because this is the beginning of our journey, not the end. So, I leave you with my personal Sage Story in that you find inspiration.

Three years ago, I told myself that I was going to make a conscious effort to seek-out women in my community and build healthy relationships. My kids were thriving in young adulthood, I had a satisfying personal relationship, my own health was good; and, I wanted more. I wanted to continue to experience the feelings and affirmations that we, as women, bring to each other. That special "something." Though I was (and remain) completely fulfilled with my small gang of girlfriends who I wouldn't trade for anything, I knew there was something else to learn from other people by reaching out. And, I don't mean a 'casual hello' over coffee, but an authentic attempt to find women who would invest as much time with me as I would with them. I'll confess though, that sometimes I mentally counted the number of times I texted or called a new female acquaintance to see if her 'return rate' matched mine. I guess you could call it my personal return on investment. Perhaps you've done the same.

In reaching out, here's what I learned. We all only have 1,440 minutes, so no matter how busy we are, our clocks tick the same. My effort. While I didn't have control over their effort, I have absolute control over mine. Was it worth calling back a time or two, or actually leaving a voice message? Yes. We're all busy. We're all making the best with what we have. Heck, we even strap time to our wrists and it glows from our microwaves and on our car dashboards. Even our phones chime incessantly with the important stuff to get done. Yes, all of us. So, cut someone a little slack when their second hand just seems to spin a little quicker. Empathize with those who feel like they never have quite enough time to make it ALL happen. It's hard. We still just have 2 hands.

I also confirmed (since I already knew this) that women don't necessarily need to solve each other's problems. We just need to listen. We are quite capable, with all our knowledge and bundle of emotions rattling around in our brains and hearts, to problem solve. Rather, what we need to do is support each other.

If my friend reaches out for a specific need, I'll hear those 4 magic words, "I need your help." Otherwise, just be there. Be present and supportive and kind. And, give a hug when it's fitting. The power of touch is just that — powerful. Embrace it - literally.

Finally, continue to listen to that inner voice. Too often, like many of you reading this, we like to guide our own ships. When that voice is challenging me, I squelch it. I know better. I'm brilliant and a problem solver. So, stop. That inner voice is our value system, moral compass, and our ability to take care of ourselves.

As we persevere through shared struggles and celebrate our successes, may I suggest you make the conscious decision to find and invest in others who can and will make our journeys richer.

I believe this. We are put here for a reason and, for many, we sit at the apex of life's pyramid. The view is beautiful. No doubt. But, as we sit here marveling at the opportunities beyond us, remember to always reach-out and help someone else, because: 1. The point is sharp, and 2. The fall is great when you go it alone. So, don't.

CARBON INTO DIAMONDS	
Reflections ... *What I gleaned from this chapter*	Personal Action Plan ... *What I plan to do with this new knowledge*

GLOSSARY

Achilles' heel: a vulnerable or weak point on our bodies represented by a place of physical vulnerability.

Alopecian: a person with Alopecia; a disease that affects the follicles of the hair. In most cases, small, round patches are bare on the head of a person. Some lose more hair on the head, face, and body.

Apocrine sweat glands: these glands release a fluid (perspiration) when hormones, anxiety, or emotional stressors are triggered. In response, bacteria on the skin's surface begins to breakdown the proteins and fatty acid in our sweat. As a result, this bacterium causes an unpleasant odor.

Avatar: the embodiment of a person or idea. For this book, avatar is meant to represent a creature from James Cameron's *Avatar* movie to represent a facilitator between humans and indigenous people from another planet.

Baby Boomer: born after World War II between 1946 and 1964 (+/-).

BMI: body mass index.

Bonobo: A chimpanzee with a black face and black hair. Usually found in the rain forests of the Democratic Republic of Congo.

Cognizant: to be aware of.

Communication (noun): the exchange of information or news; the successful conveying or sharing of ideas and feelings; sending or receiving information. Root: Latin - meaning "to share."

Confederate: in experimental research, an actor who participates by pretending to be a subject, but actually working for the researcher (also known as a stooge).

Crohnie: a person with Crohn's Disease.

Cro-Magnon: robustly built human (caveman-like) with strong, muscular bodies. Their foreheads were fairly flat with a protruding ridge along the brow line. Brain capacity: like the modern human.

Dolby stereo: trademarked for its stereo sound formats and consisting of two basic systems to help with noise reduction; in particular, in movie theaters.

Donna Van Natten's Image of Woman: based on Da Vinci's Image of Man, find the woman within and help her shine.

Duchenne Smile: neurologist, Guillaume Duchenne, identified two distinct smiles based on contractions of both the mouth and eye muscles to express genuine, positive emotions. His work has been linked to facial expressions, emotions, and a facial coding system.

Fe in Female: we are Iron tough and the Fe in Female. Know this. Live this.

fNIRS hyperscanning: technology typically used for studying social cognition. Functional Near-Infrared Spectroscopy (fNIRS).

Gam: a person's leg; especially an attractive female leg.

Gen X: the generation following the Baby Boomers. Approximately 51 million people born between 1965 and 1976 (+/-).

Golden years: the time span between retirement and the beginning of aging.

Idiom: a group of words with a meaning not deducible from their individual words.

Lexigram: a symbol that represents a word, especially when learning a language.

Mile's Law: under the leadership of three presidents, Rufus E. Miles, Jr. (1910-1996) was known for his unique perspectives and encounters with reality. He codified ideas that he believed people should intuitively know and that we form judgments from our own perspectives. He added six maxims to his law.

Pet peeve: something that a person finds especially annoying or irksome.

Polyvagal Theory: Dr. Stephen Porges's theory on the two functions of the brain, the primitive and more evolved structures, and how emotions, stress, and social behaviors impact our brain and bodies. Polyvagal is the blend of poly (many) + vagal (vagus nerve).

Purlicue: the space or distance between the thumb and the forefinger.

ROI: return on investment

Symmetry: an arrangement of parts on the opposite sides (like the face) characterized by excellence of proportion or balance.

Torso: from the Italian, meaning "stalk or stump," this is the main area of the body when arms and legs come together.

Wallflower: someone on the sideline of an activity. Typically associated with shyness or unpopularity. Commonly referenced standing near the wall at a party.

Wenis: the extra skin on the outside of the elbow. Plural: wenises.

SAGE BIOS

JANET DUNN, CEO

Janet has a 30 year professional history working for the YMCA. In that time, she has worked for Y's in Findlay, OH, Toledo, OH, YMCA of the USA (serving 27 states as a consultant for operations), Chief Operating Officer for the YMCA of Greater Augusta, and, currently, CEO for the YMCA of Metropolitan Chattanooga. Janet is responsible for a $15 million dollar  budget supporting 8 operating units in greater Chattanooga. The YMCA of Metropolitan Chattanooga employs 1,200 and has membership of more than 50,000 people.

Janet holds a BS degree from Kent State University. She is the first woman CEO serving the YMCA of Metropolitan Chattanooga's 144 year history. Presently, Janet is the only female YMCA CEO in the State of Tennessee. She serves on numerous boards and executive committees, including Chattanooga Women's Leadership Institute, United Way of Chattanooga, Chattanooga Chamber of Commerce, YMCA Blue Ridge Assembly, Chattanooga Rotary, and YMCA State Alliance of Tennessee.

Janet is a published author for the YMCA professional magazine, *Perspective*. She is married, has two adult children, and three grandchildren.

BRITTANY GRAY, MSW

Brittany serves as the Director of Planning
and Strategic Initiatives of Future
Foundation, Inc.; an organization providing
a holistic service model designed to target
middle and high school student academic
achievement and support system-level change
through strategic, multi-sector partnerships.
In her role, Brittany leads new business
development, planning, & evaluation efforts
primarily through cultivating & coordinating strategic partnerships that
support gaps in operational & programmatic infrastructure. She also
supports organizational growth through marketing, communications, and
sustainability efforts in fundraising.

Under her leadership, Future Foundation has cultivated and developed
new, sustainable corporate and private foundation sponsors to support
revenue diversification and secured over $1.5 million dollars in innovation
investments for the organization. Brittany also served as a national
conference presenter at the US Department of Health & Human
Services annual meeting in 2013 and currently serves as a member of
Future Foundation's Young Leaders Council. In her role, she connects
young professionals to professional development opportunities through
volunteerism. She also participated in The University of Georgia's J.W.
Fanning Institute's Executive Leadership Program for Nonprofit Executives
(ELPNO). Brittany earned her BS in Social Work from the University of
Georgia and an MSW from Georgia State University's Andrew Young
School of Policy Studies.

MICHELE HICKS, RN

Michele graduated from Humber College, Toronto, Canada, with a nursing degree. She started her professional career in Port Huron, Michigan on a hospital cancer ward and relieved nursing staffs in the Emergency Department. Michele applied for an opening in the operating room, landed it, and learned the required skills for the demanding, quick paced job. She moved to Canada and worked in operating rooms and intensive care units while pursuing her BA in Psychology. After 15 years of working in the operating room, she took the Head Nurse position and worked her way up to Director of Surgical Services. She continued her studies and graduate work towards a Master's degree in Business. Residing in Canada, Michele has an active, full life as a volunteer, mother, grandmother, and wife. She spends time traveling and enjoys riding her motorcycle with friends and family.

MARIANNE LORREN, CPA

Marianne brings ten years of public accounting and financial consulting experience to Henderson, Hutcherson & McCullough's Tax Department in Chattanooga, Tennessee. She previously served at firms in California, Florida, and Missouri as a tax accountant. In addition to preparing traditional tax returns for individuals, partnerships, estates, trusts, and corporations, she works with high-net-worth individuals, has produced a 50-state sales tax analysis for a national media distribution corporation, and provided financial consulting for an international  men's grooming line. Marianne lives with her family in Chattanooga and maintains professional affiliations with the American Institute of Certified Public Accountants, Tennessee Society of Certified Public Accountants, Chattanooga Tax Practitioners, and Chattanooga Women's Leadership Institute.

CURT LOX, PHD

Dr. Curt Lox is a professor of Applied Health and Dean of the School of Education, Health and Human Behavior at Southern Illinois University - Edwardsville. His research interests center broadly around the psychological and emotional aspects of exercise in special populations. Curt has served as the sport psychologist for the US Martial Arts Team and continues to work as a sport psychology consultant for players and coaches at the interscholastic, intercollegiate, and professional levels in the greater St. Louis area. Dr. Lox is also co-author of an exercise psychology text entitled *The Psychology of Exercise: Integrating Theory and Practice* which is currently in its fourth edition.

CAREY NEASE, MD

Dr. Nease is a Facial Plastic and Cosmetic surgeon, and a graduate of the University of Florida College of Medicine. He is originally from Ocala, Florida where he spent most of his childhood with his parents and four siblings. For the last 7 years, Carey has lived in Chattanooga, TN with his wife, Pamela, and their four children. He regularly performs a full-range of cosmetic procedures, but has exceptional talent in aesthetic surgical procedures for facial rejuvenation. Dr. Nease is certified by the American Board of Cosmetic Surgery, the American Board of Facial Plastic and Reconstructive Surgery, and the American Board of Otolaryngology. He has performed more than 10,000 cosmetic surgical procedures in the last 13 years, using innovative techniques with laser technology and unsurpassed commitment to excellence through surgical artistry. Dr. Nease is also a fellowship director for the American Academy of Cosmetic Surgery (AACS) post-graduate training program and is a trustee of the AACS and the American Board of Cosmetic Surgery. He has authored several book chapters, original journal articles, and is a frequent speaker at cosmetic surgical conferences across the country.

GLADYS PINEDA-LOHER

Gladys serves as the Director of International Community Outreach at Chattanooga State Community College. She was also the creator of the International Business Council at the Chattanooga Area Chamber of Commerce, founded on the need to solicit feedback from the international community. Recently, she spearheaded the "Cultural Ambassadors and International Achievers at ChSCC" which strives to increase inclusion and participation in educational programs  emphasizing mentorship, leadership, retention, achievement, and success for underrepresented groups and international local students. She serves on numerous boards, including the Office of Multicultural Affairs, Goodwill Industries, and Partnership for Families, Children and Adults. Gladys is a member of the Chancellor Multicultural Advisory Council (CMAC) at the University of Tennessee, Hamilton County Government's Title VI Community Monitoring Committee, VW Diversity Advisory Council, Arts Build, and Chattanooga Area Chamber of Commerce International Business Council.

Gladys graduated from the University of Manizales with a B.A. in Accounting, and a Master's degree in Health Care Administration from the University Javeriana - Cali. Her husband, Terry, and she have four children and reside in Chattanooga, TN. When not working, Gladys enjoys salsa dancing with her husband and hiking with her kids. She loves cooking Colombian recipes and making memories with her family and friends.

LESLEY STILES SCEARCE, CEO

Lesley was appointed President and CEO of
United Way of Greater Chattanooga in 2015.
United Way is a dynamic and innovative
nonprofit committed to addressing critical
social service issues to build a stronger and
healthier community for all. Since joining
United Way, she has been an initiative leader
with Chattanooga 2.0, a collective effort to
make Chattanooga the "smartest city in the
South," and she has partnered United Way
with new community collaborators who
bring innovation and risk-taking to solving
nonprofit issues – a recognized United Way

hallmark. Recently, Lesley helped launch a new citywide #CHAgives
fundraiser; she shepherds the use of advanced technology and social
media at the nonprofit, and most recently, successfully completed her
first community campaign. Before joining United Way, she headed On
Point as its President and CEO. Ms. Scearce led the organization to equip
240,000 local youth with skills and support necessary to avoid risky
behavior and be prepared for life. Lesley was also an adjunct professor
of nonprofit management at the University of Tennessee, Chattanooga.
She led ASCEND, in Washington DC, as Board Chair. She also leads
community wide trainings for parents, schools, businesses and community
organizations in the 40 Developmental Assets®, the building blocks youth
need to flourish.

Lesley is grateful for the investments made in her as a young adult; so, she is
passionate about launching kids towards an atypical life and transforming
the way adults view and engage with youth. When she isn't wrangling two
young boys or watching games at the ball field, you'll probably find her on
her front porch with her husband, Daniel, and their friends. She loves fly
fishing and folk music, and is an active member of Calvary Chapel. Lesley
resides and thrives in Chattanooga, TN.

SYLVIA SKREL

Sylvia was born in 1928 and is an active member of her community. She has two sons, three granddaughters, and one great granddaughter - who are the joys of her life. In 1977, she graduated Paralegal school from Madonna University in Michigan. Three years later, she was elected to the Michigan House of Representatives in a special election to fill a vacancy. Sylvia was, subsequently, re-elected for a full 2-year term.

She enjoys all sports and is an avid basketball player, ice skater, and golfer. Throughout her life, Sylvia has volunteered her time for heartfelt causes, including the March of Dimes, the League of Women Voters, and numerous political campaigns. She worked as a Constituent Representative in a US Congressman's district office and, later, she transferred to the Washington, DC area to become the Congressman's Legislative Advisor. Sylvia received a presidential appointment to the US Department of Energy from President George H.W. Bush where she worked until she retired in 1997. She currently resides in Virginia and spends her time dancing, gardening, and writing her memoirs.

RACHEL SLIKKER

Rachel has passion is to help dislocated workers get back to work, and help them truly discover their next steps for a successful future. She is an expert at individualizing plans of action for her customers because she knows that when people lose their job, they don't just lose their source of income, they lose their identity and sense of value. Rachel assists customers in understanding all their options, whether it is college courses, on-the-job training, or new employment opportunities. Rachel has a Bachelor's degree  in Business Management and has continued her passion through additional training through the Southeastern Employment and Training Association. She is a certified Global Career Development Facilitator which allows her to guide her clients through the process of identifying their transferrable skills and to help them see their full potential. Fluent in Spanish and English, Rachel is able to make cultural connections with the people she surrounds herself with daily.

DANA STARK

Dana Lees Stark has been a practicing, licensed speech-language pathologist in the California public school system for 26 years. She attended Washington State University and California State University - Fullerton, receiving both her Bachelor's and Master's in Communicative Disorders. She is an active member of the American Speech Language-Hearing Association with her Certificate of Clinical Competence, as well as her Clinical Rehabilitative Credential in California. She supervises clinical speech-language pathology  interns from Loma Linda University and the University of Redlands. Dana is a United States Pony Club graduate and alumni, and the Horse Management Organizer for the Southern California Regional Pony Club. She lives in Riverside, California with her husband and two youngest daughters. Dana is an avid horsewoman, chef, artist, and gardener.

REFERENCES

Antai-Otong, D. (1999). Communication: Active Listening at Work. *The American Journal of Nursing, 99*(2), 24L-24P. doi:1. Retrieved from http://www.jstor.org/stable/3471980 doi:1

Baker, Joseph N., Liu, Ning, *Sex differences in neural and behavioral signatures of cooperation revealed by fNIRS hyperscanning,* Scientific Reports, June 8, 2016

Bernieri, Frank J., Petty, Kristen N., *The influence of handshakes on first impression accuracy,* Psychology Press (2011)

Bookwala, Jamila, Boyar, Jenny, GENDER, EXCESSIVE BODY WEIGHT, AND PSYCHOLOGICAL WELL-BEING IN ADULTHOOD, *Psychology of Women Quarterly,* 32 (2008), 188–195. Blackwell Publishing, Inc. Printed in the USA. Division 35, American Psychological Association. 0361-6843/08

Bortfeld, Heather, Leon, Silvia D., Bloom, Jonathan E., Schober, Michael F., Brennan, Susan, E., *Disfluency rates in conversation: Effects of age, relationship, topic, role, and gender,* Language & Speech, Vol. 44 (June 2001) pp 123-147

Casey A. Klofstad, Rindy C. Anderson, Susan Peters, *Sounds like a winner: voice pitch influences perception of leadership capacity in both men and women,* Published 14 March 2012.DOI: 10.1098/rspb.2012.0311 http://rspb.royalsocietypublishing.org/content/279/1738/2698

Cheng, X., Li, X. and Hu, Y. (2015), *Synchronous brain activity during cooperative exchange depends on gender of partner: A fNIRS-based hyperscanning study.* Human Brain Mapping., 36: 2039–2048. doi:10.1002/hbm.22754

Cuddy, Amy J.C., Wilmuth, Caroline A., Yap, Andy J. and Camey, Dana R., *Preparatory Power Posing Affects Nonverbal Presence and Job Interview Performance,* Journal of Applied Psychology © 2015 American Psychological Association, 2015, Vol. 100, No. 4, 1286–1295

Ekman, Paul, *Telling Lies*, Norton (1985)

Erard, Michael, *Read My Slips: Speech Errors Show How Language Is Processed*, Science, September 21, 2007

Fredrickson, B. L., & Roberts, T. A. (1997). *Objectification theory: Toward understanding women's lived experiences and mental health risks.* Psychology of Women Quarterly, 21, 173–206. doi:10.1111/j.1471 6402.1997.tb00108.x

Gobl, Christer, Ni Chasaide, Ailbhe, *The role of voice quality in communicating emotion, mood and attitude,* Speech Communication, Vol 40 (2003) pp. 189-212, http://www.cs.columbia.edu/~julia/papers/gobl03.pdf

Goffe, Rob and Jones Gareth, *Creating the Best Workplace on Earth*, Harvard Business Review, May 2013, p 99-106

Grabe, Shelly; Ward, L. Monique; Hyde, Janet Shibley, *The role of the media in body image concerns among women: A meta-analysis of experimental and correlational studies.* Psychological Bulletin, Vol 134(3), May 2008, 460-476. http://dx.doi.org/10.1037/0033-2909.134.3.460

Graham Ph.D., Jean Ann and Jouhar M.D., A.J., *The Importance of Cosmetics in the Psychology of Appearance, Department of Dermatology, University of Pennsylvania School of Medicine*, April 1983

Grasz, Jennifer, *Swearing at Work Can Harm Your Career Prospects, Finds CareerBuilder Survey*, http://www.careerbuilder.com/share/aboutus/pressreleasesdetail.aspx?sd=7/25/2012&id=pr709&ed=12/31/2012

Gueguen Nicolas, *High Heels Increase Women's Attractiveness*, Arch Sex Behave (2014)

Gueguen, Nicolas, *Women's hairstyle and men's behavior: A field experiment,* Scandinavian Journal of Psychology, 12/2015, Volume 56, Issue 6

Gunnery, Sarah D., *The Deliberate Duchenne Smile: Perceptions and Social Outcomes,* A dissertation to the Department of Psychology, Northeastern University, Boston, MA, June 7, 2013; https://repository.library.northeastern.edu/downloads/neu:3315?datastream_id=content

Hadgraft, Nyssa T., Lynch, Brigid M., Clark, Bronwyn K., Healy, Genevieve N., Owen, Neville and, Dunston, David W., *Excessive sitting at work and at home: Correlates of occupational sitting and TV viewing time in working adults.* BMC Public Health. 15 (Sept. 15, 2015): p899. DOI: http://dx.doi.org.ezproxy.liberty. edu:2048/10.1186/s12889-015-2243-y

Harper, B., & Tiggemann, M., *The effect of thin ideal media images on women's self-objectification, mood, and body image.* Sex Roles, *(2008)* 58(9-10), 649-657. doi:http://dx.doi.org/10.1007/s11199-007-9379-x

Harvard Business Review, *Women in the Workplace: A Research Roundup,* September 2003

Howlett, N., Pine, K. J., Orakçıoğlu, I., & Fletcher, B. (2013). *The influence of clothing on first impressions: Rapid and positive responses to bespoke features in male attire.* Journal of Fashion Marketing and Management, 17, 38–48. doi:10.1108/13612021311305128

Jianga, Hua, Luob, Yi and, Kulemekac, Owen, *Leading in the digital age: A study of how social media are transforming the work of communication professionals,* a) S.I. Newhouse School of Public Communications, Syracuse University, United States, b) School of Communication and Media, Montclair State University, United States, c) Gaylord College of Journalism and Mass Communication, The University of Oklahoma, United States; Received 26 March 2015, Revised 28 October 2015, Accepted 29 October 2015, Available online 30 October 2015. Telematics and Informatics, Volume 33, Issue 2, May 2016, pp. 493–499

Johnsen Rasmus, Muhr, Sara Louise and, Pedersen, Michael, *"The frantic gesture of interpassivity",*

Journal of Organizational Change Management, (2009) Vol. 22 Issue 2 pp. 202 - 213 Permanent link to this document: http://dx.doi.org/10.1108/09534810910947217

Jung, R. E., Haier, R. J., Yeo, R. A., Rowland, L. M., Petropoulos, H., Levine, A. S., . . . Brooks, W. M. (2005). *Sex differences in N-acetylaspartate correlates of general intelligence: An 1H-MRS study of normal human brain. NeuroImage, July 1, 2005, Vol 26*(3), 965-972. http://www.sciencedirect.com/science/article/pii/S1053811905001473#

Kozak, Megan, N., Roberts, Toni-Ann, Patterson, Kelsey E., *She Stoops to Conquer? How Posture Interacts With Self-Objectification and Status to Impact Women's Affect and Performance, Psychology of Women Quarterly September 2014 vol. 38 no. 3 414-424*

Leigh, L., Robyn, R., Madelyn, G., & Jenni, G. *The inferences of gender in workplace bullying: A conceptual analysis.* Gender & Behaviour, (2014) *12*(1), 6059-6069. Retrieved http://ezproxy.liberty.edu:2048/login?url=http://search.proquest.com/docview/1658534546?accountid=12085

Li, M., Lu, S., Wang, G., & Zhong, N. (2015). The Effects of Gender Differences in Patients with Depression on Their Emotional Working Memory and Emotional Experience. *Behavioural Neurology, 2015*, 807343. http://doi.org/10.1155/2015/807343

Masser, Barbara and Abrams, Dominic, *Reinforcing the glass ceiling: The consequences of hostile sexism for female managerial candidates.* Sex Roles, (2004) 51 (9-10). pp. 609-615. ISSN 0360-0025

Matsumoto, David and Frank, Mark G., Hwang, Hyi Sung, *Nonverbal Communication: Science and Applications* Sage (2013)

Mehrabian, Albert, *Nonverbal Communication*, Aldine (1972)

Mondloch, Catherine J., *Sad or fearful? The influence of body posture on adults' and children's perception of facial displays of emotion,* Department of Psychology, Brock University, 500 Glenridge Avenue, St. Catharines, Ontario, Canada L2S 3A1 *Received 6 August 2010, Revised 4 August 2011, Available online 20 September 2011*

Morris, Desmond, *Body talk: the Meaning of Human Gestures* Crown (1994)

Mussap, Alexander J., Strength of faith and body image in Muslim and non-Muslim women, Mental Health, Religion & Culture, (2009) 12:2, 121-127

Nash, Rebecca, Fieldman, George, Hussey, Trevor and Leveque, Jean-Luc, Pineau, Patricia, *Cosmetics: They Influence More Than Caucasian Female Facial Attractiveness,* Journal of Applied Social Psychology, Vol. 36-Number 2, pp. 493-504 (2006)

Nauman, Laura P., Vazire, Simine, Rentfrow, Peter J., Gosling, Samuel D., *Personality Judgments Based on Physical Appearance*, University of California, Riverside (2010)

National Center for Educational Statistics, *Undergraduate Enrollment (last updated May 2016)*: http://nces.ed.gov/programs/coe/indicator_cha.asp

O'Connor, Jillian, Re, David E., Feinberg, David R., *Voice Pitch Influences Perceptions of Sexual Infidelity*, Evolutionary Psychology, Published January 1, 2011, doi:10.1177/147470491100900109

Payne Ph.D., Ruby K., *A Framework for Understanding Poverty*, aha! Process Press (1996)

Peluchette, J. V., Karl, K., & Rust, K. (2006). *Dressing to impress: Beliefs and attitudes regarding workplace attire.* Journal of Business and Psychology, 21, 45–63. doi:10.1007/s10869-005-9022-1

Pew Research Center, *Breadwinner Moms: Mothers Are the Sole or Primary Provider in Four-in-Ten Households with Children; Public Conflicted about the Growing Trend*, May 29, 2013 http://www.pewsocialtrends.org/files/2013/05/Breadwinner_moms_final.pdf

Phipps, Robert, *Body Language, It's What You Don't Say That Matters*, Capstone (2012)

Roberts, Craig S., Owen, Roy C., Havlicek, Jan, *Distinguishing Between Perceiver and Wearer in Clothing Color-Associated Attributions*, Evolutionary Psychology (2010)

Rodero, Emma, *Influence of Speech Rate and Information Density on Recognition: The Moderate Dynamic Mechanism*, Media Psychology19.2 (Apr-Jun 2016): 224-242

Rosette, Ashleigh Shelby and Dumas, Tracy, L., *The hair dilemma: conform to mainstream expectations or emphasize racial identity*, Duke Journal of Gender Law & Policy. 14.1 (Jan. 2007): p407. Copyright: COPYRIGHT 2007 Duke University, School of Law

Sadro, Javid, Jarudi, Izzat, and Sinhao, Pawan, *The role of eyebrows in face recognition,* Perception, 2003, volume 32, pages 285 ^ 293, Department of Brain and Cognitive Sciences, Massachusetts Institute of Technology, 45 Carleton Street, E25-201, Cambridge, MA 02142, USA; e-mail: sadr@mit.edu; sinha@ai.mit.edu. Received 23 April 2002, in revised form 4 November 2002; published online 7 March 2003

Scherer, Klaus, R., *Vocal communication of emotion: A review of research paradigms,* Speech Communication, 2003, Volume 40, Number 1-2, pp. 227-256

Skinner, B.F., *Verbal Behavior,* Copley Publishing Group, (1957)

Smith, Lindsey W., Delgado, Robert A., *Body Language: The Interplay between Positional Behavior and Gestural Signaling in the Genus Pan and Its Implications for Language Evolution,* AMERICAN JOURNAL OF PHYSICAL ANTHROPOLOGY 157:592–602 (2015)

Swayden, Keli J., Anderson, Karen, K., Connelly, Lynne M., Moran, Jennifer, S., McMahon, Joan K. and, Arnold, Paul M., *Effect of sitting vs. standing on perception of provider time at bedside: A pilot study,* Patient Education and Counseling, Volume 86, Issue 2, February 2012, pp. 166–171

United States Department of Labor, Department of Statistics, *Women in the Labor Force*: https://www.dol.gov/wb/stats/stats_data.htm

University Of California, Irvine. "Intelligence In Men And Women Is A Gray And White Matter." Science Daily, 22 January 2005. <www.sciencedaily.com/releases/2005/01/050121100142.htm>.

Vaes, J., Paladino, P., & Puvia, E. (2011*). Are sexualized women complete human beings? Why men and women dehumanize sexually objectified women.* European Journal of Social Psychology, 41, 774–785. doi:10.1002/ejsp.824.

WikiHow, *How to Expand Your Vocabulary* http://www.wikihow.com/Expand-Your-Vocabulary

Willis, Janine and Todorov, Alexander, *First Impressions: Making Up Your Mind After a 100-Ms Exposure to a Face,* Association for Psychological Science, Vol. 17- Number 7 (2006)

Zhang, K. C. *What I look like: College women, body image, and spirituality.* Journal of Religion and Health, *(2013) 52*(4), 1240-52. doi:http://dx.doi.org/10.1007/s10943-012-9566-0

http://www.freepik.com/free-photos-vectors/banner">Banner vector designed by Starline - Freepik.com</a>

INDEX

Connect With The Author

Facebook: Body Language Dr.
Twitter: @donnavannatten
LinkedIn: Dr. Donna Van Natten

Use #bodylanguagedr on any Social Media accounts to know more
about Dr. Donna Van Natten

Open Book Editions
A Berrett-Koehler Partner

Open Book Editions is a joint venture between Berrett-Koehler Publishers and Author Solutions, the market leader in self-publishing. There are many more aspiring authors who share Berrett-Koehler's mission than we can sustainably publish. To serve these authors, Open Book Editions offers a comprehensive self-publishing opportunity.

A Shared Mission

Open Book Editions welcomes authors who share the Berrett-Koehler mission—Creating a World That Works for All. We believe that to truly create a better world, action is needed at all levels—individual, organizational, and societal. At the individual level, our publications help people align their lives with their values and with their aspirations for a better world. At the organizational level, we promote progressive leadership and management practices, socially responsible approaches to business, and humane and effective organizations. At the societal level, we publish content that advances social and economic justice, shared prosperity, sustainability, and new solutions to national and global issues.

Open Book Editions represents a new way to further the BK mission and expand our community. We look forward to helping more authors challenge conventional thinking, introduce new ideas, and foster positive change.

For more information, see the Open Book Editions website:
http://www.iuniverse.com/Packages/OpenBookEditions.aspx

Join the BK Community! See exclusive author videos, join discussion groups, find out about upcoming events, read author blogs, and much more! http://bkcommunity.com/

Printed in the United States
By Bookmasters